DON'T BE CLUELESS

GARRY COBB AND PAT BRESLIN

DON'T BE CLUELESS

7 Keys to Life in the Real World

THE LYONS PRESS
Guilford, Connecticut
An imprint of The Globe Pequot Press

To buy books in quantity for corporate use
or incentives, call **(800) 962–0973**
or e-mail **premiums@GlobePequot.com**.

The Lyons Press is an imprint of The Globe Pequot Press.

10 9 8 7 6 5 4 3 2 1

Printed in the United States of America

Designed by Mimi LaPoint

ISBN 978-1-59921-258-6

Library of Congress Cataloging-in-Publication Data
is available on file.

Contents

Introduction

My name is Garry Cobb, and I wrote this book with my close friend Pat Breslin. We have put together a series of chapters that contain a lot of tried and proven methods for living successful, meaningful, and purposeful lives. We're sure that those of you who are looking to lift their spirits, enhance their vision, or energize and motivate their psyche will get more than enough out of this book, which is a fairly quick read. We had originally started out writing a book for young adults, but we discovered that the fundamentals of quality living ring true and loud to all ages. If you're grabbing a copy for yourself, I encourage you to grab one for your teenager or college student, because both of them will get just as much out of it.

It's funny, but Pat and I look like total opposites. I'm a black man who stands about six foot three and weighs nearly two hundred fifty pounds, while Pat is a white man who stands barely five foot seven and weighs about one hundred seventy pounds. We don't look alike, but once we met nearly a decade ago, we discovered that we have quite a few things in common. Neither of us lacks for energy, and we both happen to love working with and motivating people young and old, and helping them to develop their talents and abilities.

Pat and I each realize that the challenges of succeeding in a career, developing healthy relationships, raising children, and on top of all that, enjoying the ride is like nothing else we've ever experienced. We understand that our great land is dependent upon the virtue, character, and intestinal fortitude of its people. We know it's not easy to find meaning amid all the chaos in our current world, but we believe there's always a pathway to excellence; we just need to take the time to find it.

Pat grew up playing soccer in Pennsylvania's Lehigh Valley. He enjoyed a great foundation for life growing up as a youth on his grandparents' farm. He went to Allegheny College on a soccer scholarshp and experienced the joy of playing the sport he loves in a number of foreign countries. Pat became a successful businessman after school and currently has an Internet marketing company. He also started a company that allows him to travel and speak to youngsters nationwide.

I grew up in a large family in Stamford, Connecticut. I fell in love with sports when I was young and after a very successful high school career, I decided to attend the University of Southern California (USC) on a football scholarship. While there, I played linebacker on a couple of Rose Bowl Championship teams as well as on a national championship squad. I went on to the National Football League (NFL) and played a total of eleven years—six years with the Detroit Lions, three years with the Philadelphia Eagles, and two years with the Dallas Cowboys.

After my days playing football ended, I developed a career in television and radio broadcasting, working as a TV sports reporter and a sports radio talk show host. I had considered coaching but decided that my coaching should be done off the sidelines and in the schools and communities of the nation. For the past fourteen years, I have spoken to youngsters and their parents in schools, churches, civic organizations, and detention centers locally and around the country.

Again, Pat and I want you to enjoy the book. If you would like to get in touch with either or both of us to invite us to speak at your church, business, or civic organization, please go to our Web site, DontBeClueless.com.

How to Find Meaning and Purpose in Life

Garry Cobb

There's Something Wonderful about You and Wonderful about All of Us

Have you ever seen loving parents gazing into the eyes of their little baby? They admire every minute thing about that baby. Parents look at their child's skin, then they rub it. They stare at the baby's hair, then they stroke it. They look at the neck and chin, then the nose, down to the arms and legs, then the feet, and on and on. Everything is admired. Each movement, gesture, and sound is greeted with complete amazement. They act like they're looking at a masterpiece. And you ask why? Why do they act that way? Why do they get so excited about a simple smile? Why are they emotionally melting about a coo or inaudible

1

word? Why are they thrilled at each sign of a little better coordination?

The reason that parents act as if they're looking at a masterpiece is simple. I believe that all parents caught marveling at their little infant are surely observing a masterpiece far greater than any man-made creation. The human being is wonderfully created. And I believe that you, whoever you are, yes you, are one of God's greatest works of wonder. You should feel good about yourself, you are a fascinating being.

I'm not going to try to prove this to you, because this is something I believe. You're special and you should believe that. Humans are amazing in that a person can choose to dwell and think on something. It can be something good or something bad. We have a choice. I encourage you to choose to think good things about yourself and about others.

I'm a Christian, it's my belief system. You might want to consider developing or accepting a belief system. What is your parents' belief system? Do they go to a church or a synagogue? Do you? Discuss it with your family members or talk to a minister or one of your friends about their belief system. What's important in your life? You know how you got here from a biological standpoint, but on a spiritual level, why do you think you're here? Even if it's no more than to take care of children or be there for a spouse, we all need to have meaning in our lives. I'm not telling you to believe the way I believe, but I do think you need to have a belief system in order to feel fulfilled in your life. Do you believe there is a purpose to your being on this earth? I happen to think there is. Right now my purpose is to try to help you be the very best person you can be. How you make out in your life is important to me. I want to see you do well. I enjoy getting my mind off me and dwelling on your success.

Your Most Important Conversations

The most important conversations you have aren't the ones you have with your parents, or the ones you have with your brothers and sisters, or the ones you have with your friends, or the ones you have with your teachers, or the ones you have with your boyfriend or girlfriend. No, the most important conversations you have are the ones you have with yourself. You know the ones, when you lay your head on the pillow at night, when it's quiet. The ones where you are totally truthful, open, and sincere because you have nothing to hide from yourself. You know what's really happening in your life and you know what's important to you and you know what doesn't really matter to you.

If you want to be healthy and stable in your life, this is the conversation you need to pay attention to. Take a moment and think about exactly what is said during those sincere, intimate talks that take place in your head. What are the conversations about? Are they about your family or school or work? What is said in those conversations that either makes you confident or afraid? Are you honest with yourself? Are you a selfish, manipulative type of person who only cares about yourself and are willing to sacrifice anyone so that you can take care of yourself? You know how a doctor will first have patients remove their clothes for an examination. Then, if need be, the doctor will take an X-ray or order an MRI to look inside a person and find out exactly what the true condition of the patient's body is. In much the same way, you can take a quick examination of yourself by taking note of those innermost conversations.

After concluding your examination, I am going to give you my remedy for whatever ails you. It's more important that you feel and say good things about yourself rather than depending on somebody else to do it. It's not nearly as important what other people say and believe about you as what you say and believe about yourself. I would encourage you to write down some good things about yourself, then sit down in front of a mirror and say those things to yourself. We as humans can choose to think and believe whatever we want about ourselves. Why not choose to believe and think good things about ourselves? Don't take something negative someone said to you and dwell on it. Choose, on the other hand, to dwell on and believe something good about yourself. Most of us tend to do the opposite. We brush off the good things that are said about us, then focus on the criticism and negative things people say to us. Choose to say and believe good things about yourself.

For instance, I tell myself that I am a wonderful creation of God. I'm a special person who is talented and gifted. I tell myself that I'm a loving, giving, and thoughtful person regardless of whether I do everything to fulfill those words at the moment. I have learned that I will gravitate in the direction that I believe in and speak about. My mom used to always grab us and give us hugs and tell us she loved us and that we were going to do great things in our lives. I have taken over for my mom, and I tell myself that. I also let myself know that I'm a winner and I always will be one. I feast on Bible scriptures, which proclaim great things about me. I make it a point to think and say good things about myself every morning when I wake up or at night before I go to bed. It's a tried and proven method that will work if you put it to work. Do this for a month and you'll feel like a different person.

I was the third in a family of seven children. We were all born in North Carolina and we grew up in Stamford, Connecticut. All nine of us lived our first year in Stamford in a two-room apartment. There wasn't room for anything else but beds. We kids enjoyed ourselves back then; we had no idea we were poor until we started going over to some of our classmates' houses and saw how they just let fruit lie around in the kitchen. In our house, when my mom bought some fruit at the store, we ate it when she got home. My mom always told us we were special and that we were capable of wonderful things. I used to pull away from her when she would come up behind me and give me a kiss on the cheek and grab me in a bear hug. She would say, "Boy you're special and you're going to do great things in your life." I would pull away even though it felt good to get the hug and that encouragement. I can remember eating mayonnaise sandwiches because we didn't have any meat to put between the bread. We ate ketchup sandwiches and at times drank sugar water. Someone might have looked at us and said, "Boy, that family is doomed."

Well, I will tell you later about the story of how my dad went back to school and got his diploma. The kids followed along. My oldest brother, James, went to Dartmouth College and he's now a history teacher in Stamford. My older sister Theresa is a lawyer for the state of New Jersey, and she also attended Dartmouth College. As you know I attended the University of Southern California, but my dad wanted me to go to Princeton. My younger sister Marilyn attended the University of Connecticut, and she's a human resources manager for The Hartford insurance company in Connecticut. My younger brother Michael attended Cornell University, and he's a former aerospace engineer who now is the assistant director of the Rescue Mission in Bridgeport, Connecticut, which serves as a shelter and rehabilitation facility for people who are drug offenders, former convicts, and others who are struggling in their lives. My younger sister Brenda attended Bridgeport Business School, and she's working in a retail business. And my youngest brother, Tony, attended New York University (NYU) and developed a career on Broadway and in television as an actor, dancer, and singer.

The next generation is doing even better. Our oldest daughter, Allie, is pursuing a career in writing and teaching, and she recently graduated from Temple University in Philadelphia. Our son, Garry, played football for and graduated from Stanford University. He's currently completing his final year at Rutgers School of Law. Our youngest daughter, Allyse, went to Penn State University, and she's finishing up her schooling in California, while pursuing a career behind the camera in Hollywood. I have a niece who graduated from NYU. I have a niece and nephew who just graduated from Columbia University. I have a nephew in his last year at Geneva College in Pennsylvania. I have another nephew attending Miami University and another one going to the University of Connecticut.

Why the success? We were brought up to expect success. We knew we were expected to succeed, so we started expecting ourselves to succeed. It wasn't a surprise. My dad was a big proponent of hard work and self-motivation, so we were taught to prepare to succeed and to expect to succeed. My mom stressed the positive things about us.

She would always dwell on our strengths and remind us about them. It was as if some button were pushed that would start her immediately talking about our strengths. You should speak highly of your children. Expect them to do well. That may mean including positive things about them when you have the early-morning or late-night talks with yourself. You should stress their positives and not their negatives. Whatever people dwell on in their thoughts or in their spoken words will get bigger and bigger in their mind. Your mind might not be actually changing, but that's not what is important. The fact is that if you say something over and over and over, it's going to become established in your mind-set. So stress the positive with yourself, and stress the positive with your children.

Would Have Given Anything to Have Had a Big Afro

As you know, I'm African American, and during my school years big Afros were in style. If you were a black guy, you had to have a big Afro for the girls to call you cute. I did everything I could think of to grow a big Afro. Having a big Afro made me feel better about myself. I had a problem then of putting too much weight on what other people thought of me. Some of my buddies used to call me "TWA," which stood for Teeny-Weeny Afro. Believe me, it hit a nerve. I hated it. I would never admit that it hurt me during those years, but it hurt down to the depths of me. I wondered why it bothered me so much.

I started using my mother's straightening comb to take the curls out of my hair and give me a big Afro. But my hair was too short, and I couldn't take the heat that the straightening comb generated on my scalp, so I needed another method.

Then, I discovered the hair dryer. It would get the kinks out of my hair, and it wasn't as hot as the straightening comb. I used the hair dryer for nearly three months, and numerous people commented on how nice my Afro looked. I was thrilled for a while, but another problem occurred. The heat on my hair was causing it to get very dry and it was starting to break off. One day, talking to one of my sisters, I discovered that if I got my hair braided and combed it out, that would give me the big Afro. Unfortunately, I never was able to come up with an answer when my Afro started shrinking back down after sweat began to roll during baseball, basketball, or football practice. I had to follow my mom's instructions and keep my hair neat and short, and accept it.

My Big Lips

My hair wasn't my only problem. I also had trouble living with my big lips. Yes my lips are big and have always been big. My buddies would make fun of me because of them. At times they would call me "Double-Bubblicious" when they weren't calling me TWA. They would say, "Cobb, if we wet your lips and threw you against that wall you would stick." Everybody would get a big laugh out of that, but I would only laugh a little bit on the outside; on the inside I was not laughing at all. For a long time I wanted to get rid of these lips in the worst way. I thought they were the key to my looking good. I felt if I didn't have them everything else would be all right in my life. I've learned since then that it wasn't really the lips or the hair, so much as I needed to start liking myself. You need to decide to accept and like yourself. Be your own best friend.

Don't Let Your Insecurities Hold You Back

Looking back I laugh at my insecurities about my hair and my lips. Nowadays, people are having surgery to get big lips. Go figure. I don't know what you're dealing with in your life, but your friends may tell you, you have to wear your hair like this or like that. You have to look like this or like that. You've got to be rich to be somebody. You have to have a man or woman or just be sleeping with somebody to really be "all that." They may tell you that there's something wrong with you if you're not "all that."

Television commercials tell you over and over that you can only "be somebody" if you're skinny and wearing this perfume or that perfume. If you're a guy, you have to be rich or you have to look like Brad Pitt or Denzel Washington. If you're female you have to be built like Beyoncé Knowles, Britney Spears, or Lindsay Lohan. With the help of Madison Avenue advertising, millions of people get caught up in not liking themselves. They get caught up in the same thing as my mind-set in high school and say things like, "I don't like my nose or my eyes or my legs." Or, "I'm too short," or "I don't like the way I'm built." Or, "I wish I had hair like this person or that person." There's no miracle, you have to just choose to believe good things about yourself.

Chances are your thing isn't your hair or your lips, but it may be your height or your weight. It could be where you live or the way you talk. I was always gifted in sports, but maybe you're not and that's bothering you. There are millions of people involved in sports who weren't that good playing them. Have you ever heard of Stuart Scott, Bob Costas, Al Michaels, or Brent Mussberger, very successful broadcasters and involved in sports but who weren't good players? Steve Sabol runs NFL Films, which does countless videos on the league and its players, coaches, owners, and fans, but he never played in the NFL. Many of the great coaches like Bill Belichick, Bill Parcells, and Andy Reid weren't good enough to play professional sports, but they chose a different avenue. They developed careers off the field. You may love movies and not have the talent to be an actor, but your role may be behind the camera.

Maybe you have a stuttering problem. Maybe it's the fact that you haven't found out where you belong as of yet. If you're a young lady, you may feel like the ugliest person in the world. If you'll look up the biographies of some of the world's highest-paid models, you'll find that many of them grew up as ugly ducklings. You only have so much control on what's happening on the outside right now, but you can be a beautiful, loving, and giving person on the inside whenever you choose. Just like a beautiful flower, you just need to find the proper soil and sunlight for you to bloom. As I said previously and will say again, find people who value and love you and spend your free time around them, because they'll help you to start feeling good about yourself.

Maybe you were violated when you were young or you're still being violated sexually now and you haven't found somebody to tell. Whatever it is, things are not unsolvable. They can get better if you give them a chance. First of all, if you are dealing with some kind of abuse that happened to you, you need to tell somebody you trust. Tell a teacher at school whom you feel you can trust. Some things are nearly impossible to deal with alone.

You Must Love Yourself as You Are

You can wind up being your own worst enemy or you can be your own best friend. You may accomplish a lot of things in life, but one thing you will never be able to achieve is to be someone else. Your job is not to be somebody else, but to be the best *you, you* can be. The only way to make that happen is to love and accept yourself as you are. If you decide to love and accept yourself, you will tend to find yourself bonding with people who are able to love and accept you as well. If you don't feel good about yourself, you'll find yourself with people who don't really feel good about you either. They'll be the kind who will use you.

In college ball and in professional football there were always young ladies who were willing to do anything to be around the players. They are called "groupies." Many of them would sleep with the players as a way to start feeling good about themselves. They would humiliate themselves, commit their life to always being available to the player or celebrity, all for the purpose of being able to say, "I had sex with this famous celebrity," or, "I know and am a friend of this famous person." Don't make this mistake. Being a flunky or having sex with someone who is supposed to be a big deal is never going to really change for the better the way you feel about yourself. You shouldn't be willing to be used by somebody and think that being with this person is going to change you into somebody else. Feeling good about yourself is something you should choose to do. You don't need props to feel good about yourself.

Stay out of poisonous relationships in which one person uses and takes advantage of the other. If your mother or father was in one of those types of relationships, you're prone to wind up in the same situation unless you correct the way you feel about yourself before you get into a relationship. If you're in a bad relationship presently, I'd encourage you to go get some counseling. If you can't afford to go to a counselor, find an older, and hopefully wiser, confidante and talk to that person about the relationship that you're in. I think the majority of the people in our country need to be counseled about the problems in their thinking and negative habits. A relationship should make the two people in it better, and it should be filled with love and encouragement, and not be one person belittling and taking the other person for granted. I encourage you to make it a point to stay even farther away from abusive relationships. If you're the abuser or the abused, you need to get out of the relationship and go get some counseling.

Don't Live the Life of a Victim

Don't walk through life as a victim and give up your control over your life. Yes, you might be able to get some people to feel sorry for you, but you are deciding to lose in some area of your life. People feel sorry for victims because they lose. You can have somebody do something evil to you, but you don't have to agree to accept a victim mentality. People who accept a victim mentality are willfully agreeing to put someone else in control of their life. You see, a victim can't get better or get free unless somebody else agrees to change his or her behavior. Somebody may have done you wrong, but you don't have to dwell on it. You can focus on reasons you should win and refuse to give up and find an excuse.

I see too many people in our society trying to prove they are victims or losers who didn't cause their own loss. I prefer to be a winner who overcame whatever somebody else put in front of me. Playing the victim means adopting a "pity party mentality." I am ashamed to say it, but I know far too many African Americans who want to dwell on why they're failing rather than trying to find a way to win. Don't be that type of person. A person with a victim mentality will be unable to see all the positive strengths they have. They're too busy looking for somebody to blame. Many times children, regardless of their age, blame the things they don't like in their lives on their parents. They say to themselves, "If only my folks had done this or done that, I would be living a better life." It is true that the decisions your parents may have made have something to do with where you are now, but you must focus on the fact that now you have your hands on the reins.

Be thankful for where you are, and unlike the lovers of victimization, realize that you're sitting in the driver's seat of your life. If you fail to accept the fact that you're sitting in the driver's seat, then you're leaving yourself vulnerable to the choices of someone else. I see people become victims in personal relationships. For instance, if you were to fall in love with someone and say to yourself, "I'll never be happy unless she/he feels about me the way I feel about her/him," you may wind up being unhappy for the rest of your life. You should never decide to put yourself in that type of situation. Always refuse to get out of the driver's seat of your life. You can say to yourself, "I'm in love with that person but if this one doesn't love me, that's OK because I'll find somebody else who's smart enough to love me."

Doing Poorly in School Was Not Tolerated in Our Home

Back to growing up—I had quite a dilemma. My father was a huge proponent of getting a good education. You see, he had grown up in Carthage, North Carolina, which was a small town in the South about sixty miles from the capital of the state, Raleigh. My dad, Jesse Cobb, was born into a huge family of sixteen kids and was raised on a farm. One reason for the big families during those times was the fact that parents figured the more kids you had, the more hands you had helping with the crops and the animals on the farm.

My pops was allowed to drop out of school when he was thirteen because my granddad, James Cobb Sr., didn't see the value in getting additional education. Grand Pops felt if you could read, write, and count that was good enough. So Pops left school after the eighth grade. About four or five years later my parents got married and Pops saw what he thought was an opportunity in the army, so he enlisted. After being there a while he saw that the soldiers with high school diplomas were the ones who got promoted to officer. After serving a couple of years he and my mom went back to Carthage and started having kids and raising our family. My dad was having a major problem finding a good job, so he made a decision that has had a huge effect upon my life, along with the lives of my brothers and sisters, as well the lives of my children, nieces, and nephews. He decided that he was going to go back to school and get his high school diploma, and after a number of years of hard work he did just that.

We eventually moved north to Stamford and my dad, or "Deddy" as we affectionately refer to him, started out working in construction. But after a few years of working and looking for something better, he applied for, studied for, and passed the Postal Service Exam and got a job working as a clerk at the Stamford Post Office. Deddy was able to make more money, and our family had benefits. This made an indelible impression on him. So he vowed from that moment on, all of his children were going to get a high school diploma.

He would not tolerate any of us seven children not excelling in school. I emphasize that he demanded excellence. If we got too many Cs, he wouldn't let us watch our little raggedy, black-and-white television set. No, it wasn't cable or satellite. And we only had one TV, but it was all we had. At times it would accumulate a lot of static and be nearly unwatchable if you didn't hold the antenna. We loved watching our favorite shows, so we made sure we paid attention in class, studied hard, and got good grades. A C or two would also prompt my dad to continuously talk about how we were not working hard or doing our best. His harping on poor grades over and over was the worst part of the punishment.

So despite being black, I couldn't go to school and mess up. I had to do well or I would have to come home and deal with my father's discipline. Doing well in school was the decision I didn't want to make, but it was the decision that I had to make. It strained my relationship with my dad during those years because I didn't think he understood what I was going through during that time. I thought he was stupid and out of touch. He didn't care what the other black kids were doing or saying. He sympathized with the civil rights movement because my parents grew up under Jim Crow racism in the South. But he thought the rioting when Dr. Martin Luther King Jr. was shot was stupid. After all, he said, they were burning down the businesses of blacks. Pops also didn't like black guys who tried to be cool at the expense of their future. That used to set him off. He would say the one thing he hated to see was a dumb black person because that meant that individual was doomed in the prejudiced society we lived in.

The Uncle Tom Comments Kept Coming

So I had to deal with the whispering behind my back of my being an Uncle Tom. For those of you who don't know what an Uncle Tom is, it's somebody who's black and who basically is selling out the black race to obey somebody who's white. There's nothing more insulting than being called an Uncle Tom. I felt like I was doing a solo act because I didn't have anybody to talk to about this sensitive issue. It was a shameful thing. To me there was nothing more devastating than having my identity as a black person questioned. It hurt. Oh yes, it hurt a lot. Many of my black classmates bowed to the peer-group pressure and did poorly in school so they would be accepted. No one came out and challenged this devastating dynamic, which was taking its toll on black youngsters. It was a regular thing to see African American students bragging to their classmates about how they messed up on a test or cussed out the teacher.

You were regarded as tough if you didn't give any respect to the teachers or anybody who was white. I hated knowing that the "white boy" or Uncle Tom image was being forced on me because I was a good student. I let this criticism take away most of the joy from my high school experience. The fact that I had to do well in school separated me from most of my black classmates in everything having to do with school, other than the football or basketball teams. Most of my classes were 99 percent white. During my time in elementary, junior high, and high school I had a total of about four or five black students in my classes. Unfortunately, this thinking still permeates many schools with minority students. There is nothing more important in your life than your attitude. This mentality of accusing a student of acting like a white boy stops millions of minority students every year from getting an education and dooms them to poverty.

Learned to Be a Chameleon

At times I was tempted to rebel, get in trouble with a teacher, and run the risk of being disciplined by my father and messing up my future. Fortunately, I never succumbed to it, but it wasn't an easy journey through school for me. I did learn how to be a chameleon and talk rebellion around the black kids, then take care of business when I went to class. It bothered me because I really didn't know where I fit. I was angry at my dad for putting me into this situation. I had this battle going on inside about who I was. Why was I caught in this situation where I didn't fit? I would later realize that nearly all of my black classmates were sacrificing their futures in order to be accepted. Over the years I have seen them pay the price for being accepted, with lives filled with unemployment, prison sentences for selling drugs, and broken relationships with their loved ones. Very few if any of their families were intact with a mother and father. I look back and am thankful for not going that way, but during my teen years, I had no knowledge of what I was avoiding. I wanted to be accepted very badly.

Our family had moved north in the summer of 1963. I remember being six years old and in first grade at Stevens Elementary School on the west side of Stamford like it was yesterday, when I saw the biggest, baddest, toughest guy in our elementary school, Andy Johnson, walking my way in the hall. He wore a big black trench coat and everybody scurried out of the way when he came walking through. Andy had never lost a fight, and he had a big family so nobody but nobody messed with him or the Johnsons. I was big for my age and figured that one day I'd be big like Andy Johnson, so he became a role model for me. I didn't tell anybody but I always remembered any time I saw him. He was like a celebrity in the school. It was a big deal to see him because everybody said, "Don't get in Andy Johnson's way." He could beat up anybody in the school. Occasionally word would get out that he beat up somebody. In the back of my mind, I thought that one day I might be able to be like Andy and dominate the school.

About seven years later when I was in junior high school, Andy Johnson, who was then about nineteen, had dropped out of school. One summer night, Andy had gone into a local liquor store and pulled out a knife on the person working at the counter. Andy stood about six foot three and weighed about two hundred forty pounds and he was built like a huge muscle. You could imagine the fear that went through the person working at the counter. Andy demanded that the employee hand over all the money in the cash register. The person did just that but also pushed a silent alarm underneath the counter, which summoned the police.

Just as Andy secured the money in a bag and headed out of the store, he was greeted by three police cars speeding up to the scene. He refused to halt when they told him to. In fact, Andy tried to attack one of the police officers with his knife. He was shot in the head at point-blank range and died at the scene of the crime.

This isn't really a big deal in the black community because so many youngsters get involved in crime and wind up either spending most of their adult years in the penitentiary or dying in their teens or twenties. I'll never forget that my dad and his discipline saved me from that life. This is one of the reasons I tell the youngsters who get in trouble with the law that there's a better way. I tell them that God will forgive them if they ask Him to, and I encourage them to say no to a life of crime.

Don't Let Your Peers Control Your Life

This is something you're going to have to face at some point in your life. Can you stand alone and refuse to give in to peer-group pressure if you must? Do you feel good enough and confident enough about yourself so you can make the choices that are best for you? Or are you so dependent on the need to be accepted and get approval from your peers that you must jeopardize your well-being? Chances are you're not dealing with the same issues I dealt with in high school, but I stress to you that you're going to have to be willing to stand alone if that's what it must take. Your life is too valuable to waste because you feel afraid to stand alone. You should refuse to compromise your values just to be accepted. Involvement with drugs, alcohol, crime, promiscuous sex—you name it—don't compromise yourself to be accepted. All of us are tempted to go the easy way, but most of the time that's not the best way. If you learn to love yourself, then you don't have to sell out your beliefs and values to have other people like and accept you. Millions of people every day are compromising themselves, only to discover after years of doing it that they are cheating themselves and their families.

Find Out What You Do Well

Take an inventory. Find out what you do well. When somebody tells you that you do something well, write it down and keep it. Find out what you like to do. How could you be of service to your family and community? What's your passion? If you could, what would you like to do all day, each day? I was always talkative. I had the gift of gab early on as a youngster. I was also a good athlete, so looking back it was obvious that I should go in that direction.

You've got to develop expertise in a certain area. That means you need to eat, drink, and sleep it. If you want to become an expert in something you've got to spend nearly all of your time while you're awake focusing on it and becoming adept in it and at it. You must be willing to focus on an area and dig for knowledge.

I can't say enough about internship programs. Most youngsters go to school and get their education and degrees only to exit their high school and college and find that employers tell them they can't hire them because they have no experience. I encourage you to try different occupations so you can discover where you belong. Unfortunately, many times what you thought something was, wasn't really what you thought. Being an intern will give you a chance to find a profession you would enjoy.

Dwell on What You Can Do to Help Others

If you want to find meaning in your life, make serving other people an important part of what you do. People who enjoy their lives think about the needs of others more than their own needs. Most arguments and fights occur because people fight for what's best for themselves and others fight for what's best for themselves. If one person changes focus and thinks about what's best for the other person, then the fighting is over. Try to be a person who is hard to fight with.

People who dwell on themselves and their own problems leave their minds open to depression. Things are never perfect for anyone, so some people use this as a reason to despair or become depressed. I have found that the people who dwell on how they can help other people tend to have better attitudes. They look for the good in others, they tend to be more joyful and thankful for what they do have. Unselfish people don't have pity parties and "poor old me sessions." They're too busy helping other people and making sure somebody else does well.

I've heard of parents who were supposed to die but fought off death for decades because their child needed a parent. Love is a powerful force. I know you've heard of people pulling multiple-ton vehicles off their loved one. Putting other people first in your life will allow you to live fear-free because fear comes from sitting and worrying about yourself all the time. If your focus isn't on you but on others, it will allow you to live freely. If you want to transform your life, dedicate yourself to helping someone other than yourself.

A giving attitude will also help you develop solid relationships, which will give you a solid foundation for living. People gravitate to people who will listen to them and take the time to show that they really care. Is it your attitude that somebody owes you something? Or do you have the kind of attitude that makes people want to be around you? Show this love to your family, especially let your parents know how appreciative you are for what they have done for you. Give this love to your brothers and sisters.

I believe that God created us all and that we are his most precious creations. You come into the world as a separate, unique individual and you leave here the same way. And regardless of how committed your spouse, parents, siblings, and friends are to you, you will go through times when you feel all alone. Many people try to fill up this loneliness or emptiness with wealth, accomplishments, friendships, drugs, alcohol, sex, power, and so on, but none of it can do the job. I really never found meaning in my life until I accepted Jesus Christ as my Lord and Savior. I had tried many other methods of being fulfilled, but I was never fulfilled by anything else. I encourage you to give God a chance in your life and for you to accept and love yourself because He does. And I want you to know that although I don't know you personally, I love you as well and hope the best for you. I encourage you to start loving yourself.

Feed Your Mind
with Positive Thoughts

Pat Breslin

 **Did you know** that we have between forty million and fifty million thoughts a day? Alarmingly, research has shown that 75 to 85 percent of those thoughts are negative in most people. That's why becoming aware of negative self-talk is so important. Two reasons why more people are not living their dreams is that they allow negative self-talk and limiting beliefs to stop them from taking the appropriate actions.

When was the last time you seriously thought about the words you use each and every day? How carefully do you select them? Your words have incredible power. They can build a bright future, destroy opportunity, or help maintain the status quo. Your words reinforce your be-liefs—and your beliefs create your reality.

Here's how it works. Heather has a thought, such as, "I'm not good in mathematics." Now, let's remember that she doesn't have this thought only once. Oh no. She's run it through her mind on a regular basis, maybe hundreds of times in her life.

Then, Heather starts to use words that support this thought. She says to her friends, "I never do well on math exams." Heather repeats this phrase over and over in her self-talk and in her discussions with others.

This, in turn, strengthens her beliefs and it's at this stage where the rubber meets the road. You see, everything that you'll achieve in your life flows from your beliefs. So, in this example with Heather, Heather develops the belief that she's not going to be successful in her math course. This becomes embedded in her subconscious mind.

What can possibly flow from this belief? Because Heather doesn't believe in her ability to excel in math, she takes very little action, or she takes actions that aren't productive. She doesn't do the things that would be nec-essary to succeed in mathematics. And then, quite pre-dictably, she gets very poor results. To make matters worse, Heather then starts to think more negative thoughts, repeats more negative words, reinforces more negative beliefs, and gets even more negative results. It's a vicious cycle.

Of course, this whole process could have had a very happy ending if Heather had selected positive thoughts and reinforced them with positive words. In turn, this reinforces the belief that she's successful in math. As a result, Heather would take actions consistent with that belief and wind up with outstanding results.

My point is, don't underestimate the role of your words in this process. People who feed themselves a steady diet of negative thoughts are destined to have a negative attitude. It is a simple matter of cause and effect. You can't keep repeating negative words and expect to be a high achiever. And that's because negative words will always lead to the reinforcement of negative beliefs and eventually to negative outcomes.

I just recently read an article about Kent Cullers, a scientist who headed NASA's Search for Extra-Terrestrial Intelligence project. Cullers, who has a doctorate in physics, was developing software that searches for radio signals indicating the presence of other life forms in the universe.

And yet, Cullers has a physical challenge to contend with. Let me tell you how he describes it. He refers to his condition as "a trivial affliction" and "just barely an inconvenience." What is Cullers's particular physical challenge? A touch of arthritis? An occasional headache? Not quite. Kent Cullers is blind. That's right, he's blind. Isn't it incredible that someone can describe blindness as a "trivial affliction" or "just barely an inconvenience?"

By using these words, Cullers is empowering himself to achieve great things. He doesn't give any power to his limitations and, as a result, he is able to transcend them and accomplish more than those who have their sight.

What obstacles are you facing in your life right now? Imagine the power you could unleash if you saw them as "just barely an inconvenience" instead of as an insurmountable barrier.

When I speak about the importance of using positive language to move you toward your dreams, you may be thinking, "Do I say these positive words to myself or do I also say these words to other people?" You may be afraid that if you tell others about your goals, they'll think you're being conceited, and they may even laugh at you.

To begin with, use positive self-talk as often as possible. In my view, the more the merrier. After all, you're talking to yourself, so you don't have to worry about others hearing your comments. The key is that you hear the positive input again and again, and it becomes deeply rooted in your subconscious mind.

Yet, there are some instances when you can benefit by telling others about your dreams. First of all, make sure that you're speaking with someone who is extremely positive and totally supportive of your efforts. This should be the kind of person who would be absolutely delighted if you achieve this goal and would do anything in his or her power to help you. You may have a friend or teacher who fits this role, or a certain family member.

Even though I'm encouraging you to use positive words to move you toward your dreams, I'm not suggesting that you ignore the obstacles you may face, or that you discourage feedback from other people. Before embarking on a goal, you want to prepare for what may be coming down the road. Personally, I prefer to discuss those issues with somebody who is positive, someone whose feedback includes positive solutions to the difficulties that might arise.

Our vocabulary affects our emotions, our beliefs, and our effectiveness in life. For instance, let's say that someone has lied to you. You could react by saying that you're angry or upset. If, however, you used the words "furious," "livid," or "enraged," your physiology and subsequent behavior would be dramatically altered. Your face would turn beet red. You'd feel tense all over.

Here are some examples of how you can lower the intensity of negative emotions. Imagine, for instance, replacing, "I've been destroyed" with "I've been set back." Or using the phrase, "I prefer," instead of, "I hate." You can also intentionally select words to heighten positive emotions. Instead of saying, "I'm determined," why not say, "I'm unstoppable!" Or in place of declaring that you "feel OK," try, "I feel tremendous!"

Using exciting words like that lifts your spirits to a higher level and profoundly influences those around you. When you decide to use such words, you're actually choosing to change the path on which you've been traveling. Others will respond to you differently, and you'll alter your perception of yourself as well.

Let's look at your life right now. Are there any areas where you've been using phrases such as, "I can't," "I'm no good at _____," "If only I were smarter?" We all know people who make statements like these.

When you make comments day in and day out for a year, two years, you're programming your mind for failure. It comes back to your attitude. Every one of these examples reflects a negative attitude. And if you see the world though muddy water, you're going to use negative language and get disappointing results.

Fortunately, you can control your words, which means you have the ability to build a positive belief system—and to produce the dreams you have for your life. The first step is awareness. I want to look at two areas of your life that are extremely important—relationships and economics.

Do you say things like, "People are always taking advantage of me!" or "I don't have quality friends." If you do, you're literally programming yourself for unhappy relationships. Your mind hears every word you speak. Instead of saying, "I would like that, but I can't afford it," which might be true, don't say it. As long as you continue to say, "I can't afford it," you will go through your life with, "I can't afford it." Choose a better thought. Say, "I'll buy it. I'll get it." When you build up the thought that you will get it, that you will buy it, you build up the thought of expectancy. You build up your hope. Never destroy your hope.

Always remember thoughts become things. The telephone was a thought in the mind of Alexander Graham Bell before it became a telephone. The electric lightbulb was a thought in the mind of Thomas Edison before it became an electric bulb. John D. Rockefeller, when he didn't have a dime to his name, said, "Someday I am going to become a millionaire." And he did. So you must realize that the things that you want out of life are thoughts first, before they become things.

One of the problems I see as I go around and speak at schools, to youth groups, and so on is the problem of personality. Many of our troubles and difficulties come about because people cannot get along with one another. I will provide you with a great illustration to help you in this area.

Benjamin Franklin came to the strange awakening that he was constantly losing friends. He began to realize that he was constantly arguing. He just couldn't get along with people. One day, around New Year's Day when New Year's resolutions are generally made, he sat down and made a list of all his nasty personality traits. He listed them one by one. He arranged them, putting the most harmful trait at the top of the list, down to the least harmful. Then he decided that he would eliminate these nasty personality characteristics one by one. Each time he found that he had successfully eliminated one, he would cross it off the list, until he had cleaned up the entire list. He developed one of the finest personalities in America. Everybody looked up to him and admired him. When the colonies needed help from France, they sent Franklin. The French liked Franklin so well that they gave him what he asked for. Today, in almost all books, the name of Benjamin Franklin is cited as the most outstanding case of personality development. It was all done by changing his mind-set through feeding his mind with positive thoughts.

Positively charged people are not merely positive thinkers. They don't refuse to see problems, but they do refuse to let the problems control them or their emotions. They disregard the factors that they have no control over and focus on what they can influence.

To help yourself develop positive thoughts, read this exercise. Following are situations that commonly make people anxious, along with some typical negative responses.

Since negative conversations only restrict your growth, you have to convert to a positive charge to get

Situation	Negative Response
Asked to do new tasks	I don't know how
Making a speech	What do I have to say?
Meeting someone important	I can't do what you do
Starting a new school project	I will never be finished

where you want to go. Negative self-talk is a difficult habit to break. For each of the situations above, here are positively charged responses.

Situation	Positive Response
Asked to do new tasks	I'd love to learn this
Making a speech	I have a worthy message
Meeting someone important	I want to learn how you do it
Starting a new school project	This is a good challenge

The difference in language and attitude is obvious. Monitor your language. Listen to the way you respond to questions and situations. Make a conscious effort to develop a positive charge. You will find that people respond more eagerly to you.

I was in a car heading to a meeting with a friend recently and she launched into a negative conversation about how much she hated her job. She despises it. She told me and told me and told me.

She went on and on about this job and how bad it was, and finally I interrupted. I said, "If it's that stressful and it's causing you that much pain, why don't you just quit and do something else?" She replied by saying something that put her in the chorus line with a lot of other people going nowhere in their lives. "I would, but . . ."

The buts just kept coming up. Sometimes it was one of but's cousins—woulda, coulda, or shoulda. How many times have you heard one of those words or phrases used as an excuse? How many times have you heard them come out of your own mouth?

Too often, we repeat negatively charged words as if we were in a trance; in a sense, when we use them we are sleepwalking through life. We seem to be instinctively adept at finding excuses for canceling our own dreams. I think many of us would accomplish more in our lives if we put "but" and its family to rest and plugged into life.

When you don't move on life, life moves on you. It is important for you to learn to monitor your language, because by listening to yourself and changing your language, you can change your attitude from negative to positive. Try these exercises if you feel you need to become more positively charged.

You should wake up every morning and feel you are blessed and highly favored just to be alive. If you can believe you are worthy of good things, you develop a sense

1. Become a human Geiger counter tuned to negative words. Listen for the buts, couldas, gonnas in your conversation and those of the people around you. Zap those negatively charged words and phrases from your own vocabulary.

2. Remember scenarios in which you may have reacted nega- tively in the past and envision yourself responding in the future with a positive charge. For example: your teacher hands back a paper saying it is unsatisfactory and tells you to redo it. In the past you might have made excuses and blamed somebody else or certain conditions. Now you respond by thanking the teacher for the opportunity to improve it.

3. Test that positive charge. For one week, concentrate on re- sponding in a positive manner to all people and every situation. Emulate positively charged people you know. Do not criticize. Encourage. Lead by example. Look for solutions. Take life on with a positive attitude.

of purpose. We all have the power to choose whether we are going to tap into the negative lower self, or the higher positive self. If sometimes you feel you need to give yourself over to resentment, guilt, and anger, it is understandable. But if you want to be free of those dark emotions, to rise up and move on, you can do that too.

Sooner or later in your life, the Messenger of Misery is going to knock on your door. If it isn't at your door right now, it is probably around the corner or just up the street. Be prepared. It is going to happen. And by expecting life to give you a knock now and then, you can handle it as one of life's natural processes. There is no need to panic, to whine, or to look for blame. Know that it will come, and be prepared to handle it without personalizing it.

Positively charged people who fill their minds with a can-do attitude are capable of enduring even life's most difficult challenges. Associated Press correspondent Terry Anderson was held hostage for nearly seven years by Shiite Muslims, who kept him chained, handcuffed, and blindfolded much of the time. Anderson, a former Marine, was kicked and beaten and tortured.

"Often I objected, loudly and vehemently. Sometimes it worked; more often it just brought more punishment. The only real defense was to remember that no one could take away my self-respect and dignity—only I could do that," he wrote afterward.

That attitude reminds me of this small boy who was being beaten up in the back of a school bus by a bully. The bully knocked him down and the boy jumped up. The bully knocked him down again. The boy jumped back up. Finally, the bully knocked the boy down and got on top of him, holding him there. The boy struggled, but he could not move the bully. Instead, he yelled out, "You may be holding me down, but I am standing up inside myself."

I've known people who handle difficult times by becoming extremely negative. Some people never take life on because they are too busy blaming and complaining about everyone and everything that supposedly block their way.

When I encounter a moaner and groaner, I am reminded of the story of the dog sitting on a porch moaning and groaning. A man walking by asked the people on the porch why the dog was acting this way.

"Because he's lying on a nail," one of them replied.

"Well, why doesn't he get off?" inquired the man.

"Because it's not hurting bad enough," came the answer.

No doubt you have encountered people like that. Examine your attitude right now. Are you a defeatist? A moaner and a groaner? Do you always have a story ready about how life has done you wrong? If so, change your language, change your mind-set, and create positive affirmations that will get you to your dreams.

Earl Nightingale, cofounder of Nightingale-Conant, producer and publisher of personal development products and services, started the company with a book called *The Strangest Secret*. In essence, the secret is, "You become what you think about most." Think about your dream, your successes, and your abilities. Focus on what you want, not on what you don't want.

You need to focus on your dream and do whatever it takes to make it happen. However, affirming your success is a dynamic tool that can assist you in the process. It will tune your mind to see yourself as a leader, which will help you bring the dream into reality. Affirmations are a great way to reeducate your subconscious about your capacity to succeed and to stay fired up about your life.

You need to have a visual picture associated with your dream. If you make the affirmation, "I am fired up about my dream," make sure you have a picture in your head of what being fired up looks like. Or you may sense you're feeling positive and on track, knowing you're fulfilling your true purpose and picturing yourself as confident.

Whatever your affirmation means to you, get a clear vision of it mentally, so you can recognize it when you've achieved it. This is especially important when your affirmation is about a state of mind or something abstract. If you're affirming being a leader in your school, you may want to imagine yourself relaxing at a resort with other leaders you know. Imagine yourself doing something you love to do, such as golfing, swimming, or taking a walk on the beach.

Here's a direct and effective method to help you ingrain your affirmations in your conscious and subconscious mind. Record them with a tape recorder. Talk to yourself enthusiastically. You could add your favorite instrumental music in the background. Say your affirmation is, "I am healthy and wealthy." Record it with passion.

If you prefer not to tape your affirmations, that's fine. Just be sure to say them every day for twenty-one to thirty-one consecutive days. If you miss a day, start over. Whether you tape-record them or not, write them down and post them in a place where you'll see them daily.

The act of creating and writing down your affirmations sends a powerful message to your subconscious— that this is something you really want. You're starting to invest energy into making it happen. Affirmations help you move on from negative thinking patterns and adopt new thoughts and belief systems about yourself. You're taking control, rather than allowing the negative thoughts to affect you. You decide how you think and feel about yourself. You're in charge!

When you're developing affirmations for your dream, you're letting your subconscious know you are in charge of your dream. Your dream is meaningful and worth whatever it takes to make it come true. You'll be amazed how the energy in your life relates to your vision once you commit it to writing.

You must guard your mind from negative thoughts and emotions. You are in control of your thoughts, you can put a stop to a negative thought the moment it enters your mind. It this easy? No, but it is absolutely critical to your ultimate success. One effective tool for you to use is to replace worry with positive vision. Worry brings fear, nervousness, and frustration. It distracts you and keeps you from operating at your optimum level.

The problem with allowing your mind to obsess and worry over something you fear is that by doing so you can actually turn the very thing you fear into reality. Remember, your subconscious mind works hard to bring about the thoughts we focus on most.

So here's the plan: When you start to worry about something, instead of doing what most people do and imagining the worst possible scenario, begin to imagine the best possible outcome you can think of. Instead of obsessing about what could or might happen, begin to vividly imagine that what will happen is good and positive. If you do this, I guarantee that you'll begin to see good things happen and you'll eliminate the bad.

Fear and worry lose their power if you're not willing to play the game. If you're a chronic worrier or live with a lot of fear, making this one change will add years to your life. You can make this change this very moment. Simply decide that you will replace fear and worry with a positive vision for the outcome of every situation you face.

Another way to eliminate the majority of fear and worry is to live in the *now*. Most people miss out on a large portion of life because they're stuck in the past, continually reliving hurtful experiences, feeling guilty, remembering all the failures. The truth is, that now, the present, is your only point of power. Yesterday is over, it's dead and gone. Tomorrow hasn't happened. Today, this minute, is all you can really depend on. So use this moment to create the life you desire. When your mind starts to wander backward to the past, stomp your feet on the floor, breathe the air around you, and live in the moment.

If you make it a practice to deal only with problems or challenges that are facing you at the moment, you will eliminate more than 95 percent of all problems and challenges. Most of your problems are either in the past or something imagined that will never happen anyway.

Just remember, what you think about, you bring about.

Our thoughts are instruments that produce tangible results in our lives. What you think is what you are. It all begins in your mind. Your mind is a powerful tool for good or evil. You've got to choose.

According to the Bible, "As a man thinks in his heart, so he is."

The mind is a very complex computer. It was designed to be the tool that allows us to create and experience anything and everything that we could possibly think or imagine. It has the ability to create something from nothing. It's like a genie in a magic lamp. All we have to do is make the request and it will go to work to produce each and every result, as we have asked.

Your mind can only create in reality what you feed it. You can't obsess on problems and shortcomings and expect a life of positive, joyful abundance. This is one of the universal laws. This cannot be changed. What you spend your time thinking about, obsessing about, visualizing for yourself, this will be your reality. So, if you want to change your life, simply change your thoughts.

Remember that I told you your subconscious mind is like a computer. It doesn't discriminate against your dreams and visions. It doesn't know if they are right or wrong for you. It simply takes the command and goes to work at turning them into reality.

You hold the power to change your life completely. You don't have to live as a victim of circumstance or luck. However, your life will only change when your mind changes. You must control your thoughts and guard your mind with tighter security than Fort Knox has.

It's important for you to realize the power that you hold in your hands. You can choose the direction your life takes. You can take any desire that you have, create a vision for it, determine that you will have it, and it will come true. It's a powerful ability we all have. You can use it to create good things or bad—it's totally up to you.

Learn to Follow Your Dream

Pat Breslin

 **Growing up around** a farm I always remember my grandfather saying—"no is not in the vocabulary." He didn't accept excuses. He didn't care how it was. You had to bail hay and get it in the barn on those hot, humid August days—the dog days of summer. The eggs had to be brought in from the chicken coop even when there was a three-foot snowstorm. I'll be forever grateful to my grandfather for teaching me that whatever it takes, you have to get the job done.

My goal in this chapter is to help you make this a great life, to help you expand your consciousness—the focused force of your will—so that you may grow and flourish in pursuit of your dreams.

You may not accomplish every goal you set—no one does—but what matters is having goals and going after them wholeheartedly. In the end, it is the person you become, not the things you achieve, that is most important.

Always have a dream in front of you. We think of dreamers as being detached from real life with their heads in the clouds. But in fact dreaming huge dreams is one thing that successful people have in common. Another way of thinking about dreams is by using the word *goals*. Goals are dreams with feet on them, dreams you can really get to. When you set a goal for yourself, you are saying, "This is a dream I'm going to make come true."

But there is a deeper truth I want to share with you. When you set a material goal in front of you, that goal represents something beyond the material—it's not just the goal of a new car, a big house—it represents the kind of person you need to be to have those things. Now I know sometimes we get criticized for being materialistic. But God made the material world, and the material world is what we have to operate in. So material goals are an extension of who you are. I'm not saying to eliminate the spiritual aspect of your life. I'm just telling you that your dreams—what you want—are good because what you want is an extension of your becoming greater, becoming better. Sometimes you just need a basic material goal to spark you to a higher level of achievement and to a higher exercise of power in your life. So you dream.

A dream gives you a future focus. A dream constantly pulls you and pulls you to be better. I was recently driving around the lake close to my grandfather's farm and pulled off to the side of an undeveloped piece of property. There was a bulldozer on the land, and some trees were knocked down. There was a lot of mud. It looked awful. It was ugly and unappealing. It occurred to me as I viewed that property that even though it looked ugly to me, there was somebody somewhere who would look at this land and say it was beautiful. You know why? The reason is that that property is someone's dream. Someone else sees the property looking the way it will end up with that person's creativity. That individual might go there every day and visualize the kind of home that will be built on that property. It's the focus of the person's future. It's that person's dream.

I know a man who has accomplished some things in his life. He is in his sixties. We were talking, and he was recalling parts of his life and expressing his dissatisfaction with himself. I asked him why he was disappointed with his life. He said, "Because I never learned to dream dreams. My dreams were there at one time, and I just kind of let them go."

Listen, your dreams are a fence of protection against negative waste in your life. I'm talking about the waste of yourself—your talents, abilities, and your creativity. If you have dreams, and if you believe your dreams can come true, you will wake up one day and realize not only how much you've already accomplished, but how much you really still want to accomplish.

When Alexander Kroll was a young boy, he went out for football. He was so lightweight and physically undeveloped that he was wiped out the very first day of practice. He went home battered, bruised, and beaten. His mother told him to quit. He told his mom, "I'm going to find a way because I'm dreaming of football." Alex had a job, worked a full schedule, and saved enough money and bought a set of weights. In order to build up his body, Alex realized that the only time he could do it was beginning at 2:30 a.m. So he got up at 2:30 every morning, worked out, went to his job, went to school, came home, did his homework, and went to bed. He did that every day until he made the high school football team. But that was only one of his goals. He went to college and became a first team All-American. He went on to become chairman and CEO of Young & Rubicam, one of the most successful advertising organizations in the world. Somebody once asked Kroll in an interview, "What is the secret of your success?" Kroll replied, "I always have dreams that take my breath away."

Now I don't know if you have dreams like that, but I want to challenge you to make goals that will take your breath away, goals that will shock you with their enormous possibility in your life, goals that will sustain you if you want to keep succeeding.

Everybody can have a dream. Everybody. Columbus had a dream. Thomas Edison had a dream. Martin Luther King Jr. had a dream. Ronald Reagan, Ray Kroc, Bill Gates—they all had dreams. I don't care whom you name. If someone did something in the world, it started with a dream.

You've got a dream, too. Maybe you have a lot of dreams. America was built on dreams. How many times do you read about people who caught the American dream? A lot, right? But how many times do you say to yourself, "That could be me." Not as many, right? Don't kid yourself. We sit around saying, "I wish that were me," instead of, "That could be me." Then we sit back and wonder about the American dream. It's a lie, we say, it's for other people.

That's where we're wrong—the American dream exists. It's out there for everyone. But it doesn't automatically come to you just by being an American. It starts with building castles in the sky and knowing the difference between a fantasy and a dream, and finally making this dream come true. It starts not with what is, but with what could be.

Colonel Sanders, the chicken king, had a dream. He had a recipe for fried chicken that he knew people would buy, only no one would listen to him. He drove all over the country, living on a Social Security check, and got rejected more than a thousand times before somebody financed his idea. He kept at it because that was his dream.

Ray Kroc had a dream. He founded McDonald's. When he bought his first restaurant, all he wanted to do was sell milkshake machines. He was a milkshake salesman. The dream didn't quite lead to milkshake machines, but that's how dreams go. As you take action toward your dream, great things will happen.

The point is, dreams aren't just for the other guys. They're for everybody. Because if you don't try, you go through life bitter and full of regret. When that's the alternative, your only choice is to dig down and find that dream that's still inside you, drag it out of the grave you put it in. Breathe life into it and make it real.

All dreams start the same way—as a fantasy. A child shooting baskets in his driveway, pretending to be Shaquille O'Neal, is engaging in fantasy. It is not yet a real dream because becoming the next Shaquille O'Neal requires more than wishing for it. It takes much preparation along with certain physical characteristics and abilities. It's too far away with too many unknowns. That child will discover if his fantasy can be developed into a possible dream.

That doesn't mean it can't happen. It just means that when you're ten years old, you don't yet know enough to get that dream. That information will be revealed to you as you prepare for your dream. Step by step you will learn what you need to do and what is possible. Then your fantasy becomes a dreamer's reality.

That same kid who fantasizes about the National Basketball Association (NBA) can also dream about making the elementary school team. That's a dream he can see, a dream that can be realized by almost any normal kid who's willing to work hard enough to get there. Then he can dream about making the junior varsity team, then the high school varsity team, and then about playing in college.

Michael Jordan's basketball career started out that way. He dreamed about making his high school team. The first year he tried out, he didn't make it. He could have quit right there, but there was nothing physical holding him back from that dream. He kept working and made the team the next year. But that was his first dream—to make the high school team. For some of us, that first dream may not be possible. What we have to do then is act out our dream so that it is possible. If you don't have the talent to make the team, you can still be a part of it by becoming a team manager. You can get to the NBA that way—and have a much longer career than a player. The point is that it's possible for anyone to become involved in the NBA in some way. If that's what your dream is.

Dreams are real. The big goal—The Dream—is always out there. Knowing that you're preparing and making decisions that will get you closer to your dream is what counts. Knowledge comes from preparation, and preparation comes from struggle. If we do not prepare, we will not succeed. Set your goals and pursue your dreams with all your heart. If you miss a goal, don't quit, resist it! You just need to learn more . . . step by step you will win!

Say you want to be a company president, but you're just out of school and the job you have is in the mail room. You can't sit around fantasizing about what you'll do when you become president and blow off the mail room job because it's not worthy of your great talents. No, you want to put everything you have into the job. You want to be the best darned mail room employee that the company's ever had. Now, instead of being a chore, that entry-level job becomes part of your training. And you use the time you have in that job to prepare for the next step and move closer to your dream.

People who say they've never failed aren't trying hard enough. If you take risks you will never have to worry about failing and you will never be in the hunt for your dream. You must get out there and fail and persevere to attain your dream. I found out it's not bad to fail. It's good. In fact, it's necessary. You learn from failure. Failure will make you stronger and give you the information you need to reach your dream. Struggle will prepare you for success. Without struggle, there is no progress.

Michael Jordan failed in his first try to make his high school basketball team. Willie Mays failed in his first months in the big leagues and went on to be one of the greatest players in the history of baseball. Abraham Lincoln is remembered for his great debates with Stephen Douglas in his first race for the U.S. Senate and that he went on to be president of the United States. What people forget is that Lincoln failed many times:

Bankrupt in business 1831

Defeated for leqislature 1832

Bankrupt in business 1833

Elected to legislature 1834

Sweetheart died 1835

Had nervous breakdown 1836

Defeated for speaker 1838

Defeated for elector 1840

Son died 1850

Defeated for senate 1855

Defeated for vice president 1856

Defeated for senate 1858

Elected president 1860

Dr. Seuss, the greatest writer of children's books ever, failed more than a hundred times to get his first book published. Lou Holtz, one of the most successful football coaches in Notre Dame history, failed miserably in an attempt to coach in the pros. The list goes on and on. Show me someone who's succeeded in pursuing a dream, and I'll guarantee you that he or she has failed many times.

Obviously failure is a part of the process of chasing your dream. The key is that every person I've mentioned and every one else who's come back from failure refused to dwell on it and decided to move on. When we learn from that failure, we are better. We advance with new information to go to new levels.

When you reach your dream, you will realize that without all the struggle and effort, your dream is not worthwhile. You will recognize the meaning behind the fight for your dream, and you will feel total victory that will bring you more joy than you could ever imagine.

It's like when you're playing baseball and the pitcher strikes you out three times and you never touch the ball. Then you get up in the late innings and hit a home run off the guy to win the game. Hitting a home run is always great. But you'll remember that one forever because of the failure that went before it. It's why baseball players love the game so much. Even the best hitters fail three out of ten times. It's the three failures that make the seven successes that much better.

Well the reality is that if you want to catch up to your dreams, you have to do certain things. You know it. We all know it, and still we find ways to avoid taking the steps we know are necessary.

What we're really talking about here is commitment. Until you make a commitment to your dream, it's not a dream at all. It's just another fantasy full of excuses. Fantasies don't come true because they're not real and we're not committed to them. But when we make a commitment, we eliminate excuses and they become dreams, and dreams are definitely real. When you make a commitment and are willing to do whatever it takes, you begin to attract the people and circumstances necessary to accomplish your goal. For instance, once you devote yourself to becoming, say, a best-selling author you might suddenly "bump into" a literary agent or a publishing company that might offer you advice on this very topic.

It's not as if these resources never existed before. It's just that your mind never focused on finding them. Once you commit yourself to something, you create a mental picture of what it would be like to achieve it. Then your mind immediately goes to work, like a magnet attracting events and circumstances that will help bring your picture into reality. It's important to realize, however, that this is not an overnight process. You must be active and seize the opportunities as they appear.

Here's another miraculous feature of the power of commitment. You don't have to know at the outset how to achieve your goal. Sure you'll be better off if you have a plan of attack, but it's not essential that every step be mapped out in advance.

In fact, when you have the willingness to do whatever it takes, the right steps are often suddenly revealed to you. You'll meet people you never could have planned to meet. Doors will unexpectedly open for you. It might seem like luck or good fortune is smiling on you, but in truth, you'll have created these positive events by making a commitment and thus instructing your mind to look for them.

Before you get excited about waltzing easily toward your goals. I caution you that even with a commitment everything won't be rosy on your path. Life will test you to see how serious you are about achieving your objective. Obstacles will arise. You'll make mistakes and suffer disappointments and setbacks, some of which may be quite severe and even tempt you to abandon your goal.

That's when it becomes important to follow the sure wisdom of Winston Churchill, who said, "Never, never, never give up," or the advice provided by the boxer known as "Gentleman Jim," James J. Corbett: "You become a champion by fighting one more round." If you've made a commitment to accomplish a goal, you can overcome temporary defeats and you will triumph.

I read an article in a magazine about best-selling novelist David Baldacci, the author of the immensely successful novels *Absolute Power, Total Control,* and *The Winner.* Millions of copies of his books have been sold.

Let me assure you, however, that Baldacci was no overnight success. His accomplishments and financial achievements were the result of his total commitment to developing his talents as a writer. Baldacci started out as a lawyer. He started law school in 1983 and didn't give any thought to becoming a best-selling novelist. He simply enjoyed writing.

Yet at the outset, Baldacci knew that he didn't have the necessary writing skills. So he made a commitment to learn the craft of writing. For the first five years, he didn't finish any of his projects. Every day, he just worked on characters, plot development, and other writing basics.

At the time, he was a practicing lawyer, and he and his wife had two young children. When did he find the time to do the writing? Baldacci worked on writing every night from 10:00 p.m. until 2:00 a.m. Now that's a commitment to do whatever it takes!

After ten years of writing, Baldacci had completed some short stories and a few screenplays. His total sales: zero. All that he had to show for his efforts were a lot of rejections from editors. In 1996 all of Baldacci's efforts paid off big time! He received millions of dollars for the literary and movie rights to his blockbuster thriller *Absolute*

Power. Such is the power of a person committed to following a dream.

I'd like to share another story with you about Benjamin Roll. In 1990 at the age of sixty-seven Roll graduated from law school. Naturally, before practicing law he had to pass the California bar examination. On his first attempt at the examination he failed. On his second attempt he failed. And he failed the third time, the fourth time, the fifth time, the ninth time . . . the twelfth time, the thirteenth time. Let me add one important fact. The bar examination is given only twice each year. So at the time of his thirteenth failed attempt, Roll was seventy-three years old. Most people would have quit, but not Benjamin Roll.

He took the exam for the fourteenth time, and he passed. In 1997, at the age of seventy-four, Roll was admitted to practice law in the state of California. Now here's a guy who was committed to following his dream. As Roll explained, "I was going to pass that cotton-picking exam if I lived long enough. And I did."

Does this story tell you anything about the importance of attitude in chasing your dream? Most people wouldn't even consider starting law school in their sixties. Yet, here's someone who not only enrolled in law school, but was willing to spend six years after graduation studying to pass the bar exam. That's where commitment separates the winners from the losers. If you're really committed to your dream you're going to hang in and prevail no matter what. And if it takes a little longer than you thought, so be it. Those who aren't committed to their dream are going to give up when things don't go their way.

The key is to keep failing your way to success and achieving your dream. Before any great discovery in the field of medicine, or any healing of physical ailments, there is one common element—all have been preceded by failure. Scientists, doctors, business leaders all had failures before they had success. But the other thing they have in common is, they did not give up.

What joy would there be if the journey to our achievements was just a luxury cruise? Absolutely none! Great joy comes out of struggle and achievement—that feeling of self-worth one gets doing what others couldn't do or said was impossible. When they failed, they didn't give up. Endurance is one of the greatest qualities in non-quitters. Develop the ability to be like a rubber ball, and keep bouncing back. With ordinary talent and extraordinary perseverance all things are attainable.

Another example of somebody who showed amazing perseverance in chasing his dream is the highly successful radio personality Rush Limbaugh. For years, Limbaugh worked at low-paying jobs and was ridiculed before he made a successful breakthrough. After floundering in radio for twelve years, he was urged to get out of the business. In 1979, he left the radio industry and spent five miserable years in a sales job he wasn't suited for. In 1984, he returned to radio, and the rest, as we know, is history. Today Rush Limbaugh has the largest talk show audience on radio as well as on television, with twenty-two million listeners on a daily basis.

So when you get right down to it there is no such thing as failure—there are only results, some more successful than others. Failure doesn't mean you've reached the end of the line and that success isn't possible. The only time success is impossible is when you quit. Quitting is final. But continued attempts with commitment and diligence can be turned into success.

In a recent television interview, singer Céline Dion was asked if she ever dreamed at the start of her career that some day she'd sell millions of records and be on tour, singing in front of thousands of people each week. The singer replied that none of this surprised her, as she had pictured the whole thing since she was five years old.

She was not bragging and has worked unbelievably hard to earn every bit of success. What she learned at an early age was her ability to tap into the power of holding a vivid, powerful image and to picture the star she wanted to become.

World-class athletes also incorporate the power of imagery to reinforce in their mind exactly how they want to perform. Whether it's a figure skater completing a difficult jump, a tennis pro attacking his opponent with a perfect serve, or a golfer driving the ball long and straight down the fairway, many top competitors mentally envision a successful outcome before actually achieving it in the real world.

Where do these pictures come from? Well, we begin to develop our "mental movies" early in life. If we were criticized or felt unworthy as youngsters, we record the events or images in our minds. For example, you may still hold a vibrant image of being criticized by a teacher in elementary school. You felt humiliated in front of the whole class. Later on when you were tempted to offer your opinion in school or to a group of people, you held back and kept quiet, all the while remembering (even if only on the subconscious level) how painful it was when you were criticized. The picture remains in your mind and exerts tremendous influence over your present actions.

It doesn't serve you to deny what happened in a past experience, no matter how painful or disappointing. You can't, for instance, change the fact that you were criticized by the teacher. You can, however, alter your interpretation of the event.

We can create new mental movies whenever we choose to do so. And when we develop and concentrate on new images of dreams, we'll act in ways that support those new pictures! So the first step is to create an image of your desired outcome. You are limited only by your imagination.

It's extremely powerful to formulate images of successful outcomes—and to run them through your mind. But there's another technique you can use to accelerate your success. You can create visual aids to move you toward what you want.

In 1990, while he was still relatively unknown, comedian Jim Carrey wrote a check to himself for "10 million dollars for acting services rendered." The check was postdated Thanksgiving 1995. As Carrey explained, it wasn't about the money. He knew that if he was making that much he'd be working with the best people on the best material. Carrey earned $8 million for his work on *Ace Ventura: Pet Detective* and *The Mask*. Then in late 1994 he was paid $7 million for his role in *Dumb and Dumber*. In 1995 he earned many more millions and is now reportedly getting $20 million per movie.

Carrey's postdated check exercise is a great example of the power of the subconscious mind to actualize a goal that is held with deep conviction and feeling. Thinking about your dream and forming images in your mind will go a long way to creating the success you desire. However, when you also use a tangible representation of your goal (such as a check), your chances of attaining your dream are even greater.

Near the turn of the twentieth century, an energetic young man named Frank secured a job as a clerk in a hardware store. As he learned the business he saw that there were thousands of items in the store that the customers seldom asked for. He knew it didn't make sense to keep this outdated inventory, for it was taking up valuable shelf space.

He proposed to his boss that they hold a sale and clear some of it out. The boss reluctantly agreed to a small sale. Frank marked the outdated inventory down to ten cents. The sale was such a success that the boss agreed to a second sale. It too was a tremendous success.

This gave Frank the idea of starting a store that sold items that cost either a nickel or a dime. The clerk approached his boss with the idea that he would run the new "five-and-dime" store if the boss would put up the capital. The boss flatly refused on the grounds that it wouldn't work. Naturally the clerk was disappointed, but he was convinced his vision of a five-and-dime store would work. Several years later he managed to save enough money to start the store on his own.

To make a long story short, Frank's first store became a huge success, and he expanded his vision until he had opened thousands of five-and-dime stores all across the United States and Canada.

You see, Frank became better known as F. W. Woolworth, and his chain of five-and-dime stores— Woolworth's—became a household name in the early to mid-1900s and made him one of the wealthiest men in America.

I tell you the story to illustrate the power of capturing a vision and following your dream. Frank had the vision to see his successful five-and-dime store long before he had the money to start it up. And he had the vision to see thousands of these stores all across the continent long before the concept of a retail chain store even existed. His boss, on the other hand, lacked vision. All he could see was the here and now—namely a little hardware store on the corner of Main Street USA. His lack of vision cost him the opportunity to share in the enormous profits of the Woolworth's empire.

We are setting ourselves up for disappointment and failure if we set sail in life without a dream. We must take time and develop our dream because without a dream we don't know where we're headed and are therefore preordaining our defeat.

That's why I say your vision is your gateway to life. When you have a big, clear dream, you don't see the walls in your life as impasses. That's what Stephen Covey, author of the best-selling *The 7 Habits of Highly Effective People*, means when he talks about "starting with the end in mind." If you start knowing ahead of time where you will end up, you'll find a means to get there, one way or the other.

One of life's greatest ironies is the fact that some of the greatest dreams are born out of adversity, proving once again that when one door closes another door opens.

Take a look at this list of some famous visionaries who molded their visions from the ashes of adversity:

- A widower with a son loses his job at a department store and envisions the day when he will own his own store and be his own boss. His name is George Kinney, founder and president of Kinney Shoes.

- Two lifelong entrepreneurs start a business in the basement of their homes with a vision of revitalizing free enterprise throughout the world. Their names? Rich DeVos and Jay Van Andel, the cofounders, and billionaires, of the Amway corporation.

- A young athlete living in a government-funded housing project in Pennsylvania envisions escaping the misery of the coal mines by becoming a football star. His name is Mike Ditka, a pro football Hall of Fame inductee and a Super Bowl champion head coach.

- Two tinkerers set up a shop in a garage with the vision of growing a business that is on the cutting edge of the information age. Their names? William Hewlett and David Packard of Hewlett-Packard, the information technology corporation.

- A young man's older brother is shot down in World War II and the younger brother eases his loneliness by listening to the radio. He envisions one day becoming a radio announcer. His name: Dick Clark, world-famous radio and TV announcer.

> • A general practitioner sees himself performing a surgical procedure that everyone says can't be done. His time is limited because he suffers from rheumatoid arthritis that will one day prevent him from operating. His name: Dr. Christian Barnard, the surgeon who performed the first successful human heart transplant.

These examples and thousands more like them of people who achieve their objectives every day of the week prove that great things are accomplished as the consequence of great dreams and that great dreams can crystallize from adversity if people are willing to follow their dreams.

One of my favorite stories about the power of following your dream concerns a man named Marty Roberts. Marty was the son of an itinerant horse trainer. As a result, Marty spent most of his school-age years traveling with his family from one farm to another. His education as a consequence was disjointed at best.

He did, however, manage to graduate from high school, and in his senior year Marty was required to write a paper on his dreams and aspirations for life. He took the assignment very seriously and he poured his heart out into the paper. He shared his vision of a two-hundred-acre ranch with a four-thousand-square-foot house. He even provided diagrams of both. He was as proud of his paper as any school project he ever completed.

Can you imagine Marty's shock when his paper was returned with a big red F scribbled across the top? He immediately approached the teacher inquiring why his paper had received a failing grade. The teacher told the crestfallen young man that he failed the paper because the content wasn't realistic. After all, the teacher noted, Marty was the son of an itinerant horse trainer. He had no money and no resources. He didn't have the capital to purchase land or to build buildings or to buy horses and breed horses, which meant, in the teacher's narrow mind, that Marty's paper was more fantasy than reality.

The teacher instructed Marty that in order to get a passing grade, he would have to rewrite the paper. Marty went home and told his parents what had happened and asked for their advice. His father responded, "Marty, it's up to you." The next day Marty told the teacher that he would keep his F because he wasn't going to give up on his dream.

Fortunately Marty's vision outlasted the teacher's cynicism, for today Marty Roberts owns a two-hundred-acre ranch with a four-thousand-square-foot home. Mounted over the fireplace in an elegant frame is the seven-page paper in which Marty first described his dream.

If Marty's story ended right here, you'd have to say it was a happy ending. But it gets even better. Marty's vision included love and forgiveness, and to make his vision complete, years later he asked the teacher who gave him the F to run a summer camp for youths at Marty's ranch. The teacher graciously accepted the offer and the two men healed the breach between them. Marty wasn't the only student the teacher had injured with his cynical attitude.

The teacher confessed, "I've stolen many young people's dreams through the years, and I'm ashamed of it. I've taken away something that would have enabled them to become what they could become. But I praise God that you didn't allow your vision to be taken away." These two men are living proof that a powerful dream can touch and change more than just the person who created it. Marty's dream changed his future in the world, but in the process it also changed a teacher's view of the world, as well as the views of hundreds of campers and students who would come under the teacher's influence.

I would like to wrap up this chapter with a statement by one of the greatest Americans of all time, President Theodore Roosevelt, from "Citizenship in a Republic," a speech delivered at the Sorbonne in Paris, April 23, 1910. Have fun in the pursuit of following your dream.

> *The credit belongs to the man who is actually in the arena, whose face is marred by dust and sweat and blood, who strives valiantly, who errs and comes up short again and again, who knows the great enthusiasms, the great devotions, who spends himself for a worthy cause; who, at the*

best, knows the triumph of high achievement, and who, at the worst, if he fails, at least fails while daring greatly, so that his place shall never be with those cold and timid souls who know neither victory nor defeat.

Establishing Goals

Pat Breslin

 **In the previous chapter,** I talked about pursuing the dreams that you have for your life. This chapter is focused on how to establish goals in order to see your vision, your dreams for your life, happen. Your goals are extensions of your dream for your life and reflections of your talents, interests, and values.

Unless you devote some thought toward creating truly meaningful goals, it does no good to set goals. For example, a car thief has goals, so does Pope Benedict. The difference is found in the quality of their personal vision and focus.

I majored in history when I was in college and loved to study great American leaders. One of my favorite historical figures was Abraham Lincoln. Lincoln became a great and effective leader by establishing goals and having them accepted by subordinates. Goals are essential in unifying people, motivating them, and focusing their talent and energy. Lincoln, as the president of the United States, united his followers with the "corporate mission" of preserving the Union and abolishing slavery. Lincoln's objective became firmer with the onslaught of the American Civil War. Even so, Lincoln realized that the attainment of a successful outcome had to be accomplished in steps, that is, setting goals. Therefore, Lincoln constantly set specific short-term goals that his generals could focus on intently and immediately. Early in the war, Lincoln created extremely strategic objectives such as blocking key southern ports, gaining control of the Mississippi River, and rebuilding and training the military. Throughout the war, Lincoln concentrated on the destruction of General Robert E. Lee's army, as opposed to the capture of the Confederate capital. Lincoln took one battle at a time rather than trying to win them all at once. Toward the end of the war, Lincoln's strategy was to set the stage for a peaceful and smooth restoration of the Union. Lincoln was always working toward achieving goals and objectives. Like all great leaders, Lincoln was driven. He was goal and results oriented.

Setting clear goals is the most significant characteristic that separates those who achieve from those who don't. A well-known ancient proverb states, "He who fails to plan, plans to fail." Even if we have the noblest and most appropriate dreams, our chances of accomplishing them are remote without proper planning.

Abraham Lincoln's commitment to planning, more than genius, was probably the factor that enabled him to conquer rival generals, restore the Union, and, ultimately, end the Civil War. Lincoln studied incessantly. He pored over maps of potential battlefields and listened carefully to intelligence reports of the disposition and strength of the enemy. Lincoln even studied the character and personal histories of the opposing generals.

Setting goals is both an art and a discipline. Even the greatest artist must develop his or her skills. Similarly, a leader must develop the ability to plan. Effective planning and goal setting requires the ability to gather and organize facts concerning the realities being dealt with. It is then necessary to observe facts in a way that will produce insights that will lead to advantage and success. I will break down the process in three simple steps.

Stating the goal:
Planning requires an ability to first visualize the future and then make a road map for navigating it. We will never know where to direct our path if we do not know our destination.

Obtaining and organizing the necessary facts:
The ability to do research is a significant skill within itself. First, we must determine where we can obtain the most accurate facts relevant to our goals to assist us.

Making the plan:

The first step in making a good plan is the acknowledgment that the plan can be changed. Therefore, you should not worry about making a perfect plan because you should be able to make adjustments as you go, if necessary. My friend Larry is a pilot and he always has to file a flight plan before any departure, but many times changes in weather or other conditions forces him to alter his plans. He quickly recognized that the knowledge of when and how to adjust his plan was just as important as making it. He found that a plan's chief function was to get him off the ground and headed in the right direction. That is the nature of many of our plans, but it is important to note that without goals we will not even get started.

A dream without a goal is similar to taking a road trip without a road map. You will definitely arrive somewhere, but where will that be? To make certain that you achieve your dreams, set specific, measurable goals that are compatible with your dreams. Break down goals into small steps, review them daily, and revise them regularly. List activities that will help you attain your goals. Develop a detailed, scheduled plan of action, and then take one small step at a time to move toward your goals. Later in this chapter, I will provide you with seven guidelines for goal setting that will assist you in achieving your dreams.

Henry David Thoreau said, "If one advances confidently in the direction of his dreams and endeavors to lead the life which he has imagined, he will meet with success in uncommon hours." You can strengthen the belief that your goals will be reached by acting as if they have already been met.

In my frequent travels to and from meetings and events, I've had the opportunity to see countless hitch-hikers who are always thumbing a ride to another desti-nation. Strictly between us, I've picked up one or two over the years—but please don't tell my mom. Some of the hitchhikers would have signs to help flag down a mo-torist headed toward their destination. One sign might read Philadelphia, while another might read New York. On one particular occasion, I passed by a hitchhiker holding a sign that read Anywhere. He did not know where he was going, but he knew that he wanted to get away from where he was.

Like the hitchhikers, we too arrive at crossroads in our own lives every day. Some of us know exactly where we are going because we have clear goals in our lives. These goals enable us to position ourselves in the direc-tion we desire. They serve as signposts that might state College Degree or Better Health or Financial Freedom.

Sadly, most people do not set goals for themselves, and the consequence is that they find themselves holding signs that say Anywhere, which indicates that they will settle for any destination. We should feel sorry for these people because they are positioning themselves for failure.

It should be obvious that it is necessary to know your destination in order to properly position yourself for success. It's not rocket science, it's common sense. I am continually amazed, however, at the number of people who do not take control of the direction of their lives by simply sitting down and writing down their goals. Positioning yourself in order to accomplish your goals may be the single most powerful activity you can undertake to achieve your dreams.

To illustrate my meaning, I'd like to tell you a story about what happened many years ago to a man named Charles Schwab. Mr. Schwab was the president of Bethlehem Steel, the company where my grandfather worked for forty-one years. A business consultant named Ivy Lee informed Schwab that he had a simple plan that would enable Schwab to run his business more efficiently, from the top executive to the employee on the lowest rung of the company's totem pole. Lee was so confident that his plan would work that he left his compensation totally up to Schwab. Lee only asked that Schwab send a check for the amount he felt that Lee's service was worth.

Being a shrewd businessman, Schwab agreed and Lee revealed his plan. It was simple, at the beginning of each day each manager and employee would make a list of the things that needed to be completed that day. The employees would then prioritize these tasks in order of their importance. They would then begin working on the first item on the list and would not proceed to the next item until the previous one had been completed. As soon as employees arrived at their desk each morning their first task was to take a few minutes to draw up a daily list with the unfinished business from the previous day placed at the top.

This basic exercise forced people to write daily goals and manage their time more effectively. As a result, within a few months, productivity at Bethlehem Steel skyrocketed and Schwab sent Lee a check for $25,000, an amount that was worth fifteen times what it is worth today.

The habit of making daily preparation is a common characteristic of many winners I have met and spoken with over the years. John Naber is one person who immediately comes to mind. In high school, John would swim daily from 5:00 to 7:30 a.m., then later from 4:00 to 6:00 p.m. Every other day he spent thirty minutes lifting weights. John's dream was to go the Olympics. Anyone who makes it to the Olympic trials has devoted much of his or her life to developing an athletic skill. Only a very small percentage of those who aspire to compete in the Olympics make the Olympic team. John once told me that "in swimming you are basically racing against the clock." He said that he would try to improve speed by .01 or even .001 of a second each time. John would then add those amounts of .3 seconds or .12 of a second daily. He also said that he would practice visualization methods while racing the clock. John would imagine the cheers from the crowd and the chill of the cold, gold medallion against his chest.

John's goal fueled the phenomenal level and consistency of his daily preparation. By age twenty, John made it to the 1976 Olympics in Montreal where all of those years of setting and pursuing small goals finally paid off. John won four gold medals. Consistent daily preparation reaps large dividends for those individuals who make goal setting a part of their lifestyle.

One characteristic of functional goals is their ability to allow you to focus on where you want to be at each step of your journey. Therefore, as you proceed, you can always determine how far you have come and how much farther you have to go. Your goals move you along and they also confirm your mission as you go. These goals add meaning to what you are doing and they provide you with a strong sense of control over your life, which your friends and family members will notice. Now I would like to lay down the seven guidelines for goal setting that I promised to provide earlier in this chapter. Here they are:

1. Goals must be realistic.

Just as your vision for a better life should be well grounded in reality rather than fantasy, your goals must be attainable. They should also be designed to build gradually, so that the more difficult goals are positioned closer to the end of the journey after you have built up confidence and determination by accomplishing earlier goals. For example, if your dream is to start your own business you would not make leasing office space in Trump Tower one of your early goals.

2. Goals must be meaningful.

The goals that you set must be focused on your vision. You should not set goals that do not have a definite direction. Many people set goals, yet many fall short of those goals because they do not construct goals that have real meaning for their lives. Every New Year's Eve people set lofty goals to exercise more and get in shape. Typically by mid-February, the state-of-the-art, very expensive exercise contraption that they purchased is serving as an equally expensive clothing rack. The individuals who are the exception to this annual trend usually make the goal to get in better physical shape a part of a greater vision for their lives.

3. Goals must be well defined.

When people set out on a trip, you don't usually hear them say, "Sometime soon, I think I'll go a couple of hundred miles to the northeast somewhere and get there whenever I get there." When you set goals in your journey through life you need them to be well defined. "I want to make a lot of money" may be a large part of your vision, but it is not a well-defined goal. A well-defined goal might be, "Within the next six months, I am going to apply to twenty different colleges and universities and be accepted by the majority of those schools." Another example could be, "I am going to volunteer to be involved in the Junior Achievement program at my school so that I can gain an understanding of the business world."

4. Goals must excite you.

I place the emphasis on you because this is your vision for your life. People around you may have good intentions in the advice that they offer you, and while it is wise to listen and consider much of that advice, you should never allow that advice to deter you in your journey. Many times this advice, while well intentioned, may be more in line with another's vision for your life more so than your own.

5. Goals may need fine-tuning.

Realistically, unexpected obstacles and circumstances may arise as you pursue your vision for your life, therefore, your goals may need some fine-tuning along the way. Keep your vision in mind and make adjustments as you progress so that you continue to stay on target. When I was in college, I figured that when I graduated, I would try to get into a corporate environment where I could spend my entire career. I had this vague goal in mind, but I did not know then how the process worked. Since I was not a business major and I did not have any mentors I was still searching when I graduated from college. As time passed, my goal changed because I developed a bigger dream of having my own business. I learned that it is very important to stay focused on your goals at all times and by doing so I was better able to make adjustments as needed.

6. Goals require positive action.

The primary purpose for setting goals is to motivate you in the right direction. There is really no reason to set goals that do not challenge you to take action. A statement such as, "I am going to consider losing some weight" is not a goal. A statement such as,

"At 6:00 a.m. tomorrow, I am going to jog four miles" is a goal. Setting goals within each of the major areas of your life, acting upon them, and then achieving them not only moves you forward but also builds your confidence in your ability to pursue your vision for your life. Goals help you act on your dreams rather than just wishing or hoping for them.

7. Goals should not isolate you.

Sometimes when setting goals and establishing a vision for your life, you may focus so intensely on where you want to go that you forget to consider what you want to become. I am sure that you have heard the saying, "Be careful what you go after because it may get you!"

I know of a very intelligent woman whose goal was to become a surgeon. She set her mind on that goal as a girl, and since high school she pursued it. The problem that she encountered was the fact that she grew so obsessed with her goals that she neglected many other aspects of her life. This young woman never formed close relationships because of their potential to distract her from her studies. She rarely attended family functions or any other social gatherings. Eventually, she reached her goal of becoming a surgeon, but she now has no life outside of work. As a result, her life is one dimensional. She is now a successful yet lonely woman because she failed to prioritize the personal areas of her life. Your relationships and your personal life should never be secondary considerations within the vision that you construct for your life.

As I have said before, your goals should serve as the road maps that guide you and illuminate the many wonderful possibilities for your life. Life becomes meaningful when you become motivated, set goals, and strive for them with determination. Goals help you channel your energy into action. They place you in charge of your life.

Goals provide you with a purpose for directly engaging in life. People who live without goals have no purpose, and even their body language is evidence of the low self-esteem that they maintain because of a lack of purpose. These individuals are on permanent idle mode, they slouch, and their conversations dawdle. They telephone with greetings such as "Hey, I'm just calling, I wasn't doing anything, so I thought I'd call you." Well, don't call me. I've got things to do.

Many people just muddle through life. They do not read informational material and they don't even pay attention to the television programs they watch. If you were to ask them what they were watching they often mumble incoherently, "Nothin'."

What are your goals for your future? What goals do you have for your relationships? Do you have any goals for your spiritual life? Develop a schedule for the next month. Then expand this schedule to the next six months, then the next year, five years, and so on. Write this schedule down on paper. Go for it!

Learn to
Seek Mentors

Pat Breslin

 **Mentoring can be** likened to taking something old and something new and combining them. At thirteen years of age, Michelangelo was assigned as an apprentice to Domenico Ghirlandaio. Michelangelo learned techniques that he would later use in painting the Vatican's beautiful Sistine Chapel. This sort of mentorship relationship can be traced to some of the earliest and most prosperous human civilizations of ancient Egypt and Babylon. These mentoring relationships guaranteed that societies would always have enough craftsmen available to fulfill the needs of the community.

The Bible is an ancient text that provides numerous examples of successful mentoring relationships. As a young man, Joshua learned how to lead the Israelites through following Moses. Timothy experienced a similar relationship with the apostle Paul. Each one of these young protégés went on to become marvelous men of great historical importance within their own right as a direct result of a mentoring relationship. Mentoring truly allows people to embark upon a journey that will take them down advantageous paths.

I recently read a book by Fred Smith, the founder of Federal Express, titled *You and Your Network*. Smith states in his book that he wanted to sing in a metropolitan opera company. One day an older friend said to him, "Fred, you have everything except talent, and without that, all the practice, discipline, and hope will not accomplish what you want. So, I suggest you find another field." Although these words were initially painful, Smith listened and changed his direction to business. That is where he blossomed and became one of the most successful businessmen in the last forty years in America. Fred Smith credits much of his success to the fact that he had a mentor who was willing to be both honest and encouraging.

I often ask people who their compasses in life have been. Your compasses, or your mental, emotional, and character guides, along with your acquaintances, provide a fair assessment of the type of person you are now and will eventually become. After all, iron sharpens iron, but lead will send you sinking fast.

When I was a child, my grandfather was a vital influence in my life. My father died when I was three years old, and my grandfather became a significant mentor to me. He taught me many things while I was growing up around our family's farm that have shaped my adult life. People, such as my grandfather, who have shaped my life or your life positively and significantly are called mentors. I often wonder who will shape the lives of people in generations to come? Who will be the molders of a new generation of people in fields such as business, law, the church, and community life? Without mentors we face a very bleak future.

Many people do not understand the importance of mentoring, but the benefits are great. Mentoring affects both the mentor and the mentored. A sense of significance is gained along with a close interpersonal bond that will last a long time. Such bonding causes both parties to find significance in each other.

Mentoring expands and creates growth in you. Mentoring relationships develop you socially, mentally, physically, and practically. In short, these relationships increase your effectiveness as a person. They hold you accountable for your gifts and your potential. In many cases mentors feel a strong responsibility to help you develop your potential. For most of us, our lifestyle, dreams of success, values, actions, and habits are all modified for us by others. All humans imitate and follow an example, even when they try very hard not to.

Mentoring is, first and foremost, a process. It arises when an individual who has a great deal of knowledge about a particular enterprise is willing to share that knowledge with someone else who shares the interest in the subject but lacks the knowledge. Every one of us can be a mentor to someone else by enriching other people's lives with our proven skills and abilities. We mentor when we create opportunities for these people that they might not have access to otherwise.

In 1919, a young man recovering from terrible injuries suffered in World War I in Europe rented an apartment in Chicago. This man decided to live close to the house of Sherwood Anderson, the famous author, who had written a highly acclaimed collection of short stories. Anderson had the unique talent to really help young writers develop their skills. These two men became very close friends. They would share meals, walk together, and discuss writing. The younger man often brought samples of his work to Anderson, who at times responded with some very strong critiques. Despite this criticism, the young writer never lost his enthusiasm. Each time he would listen and take notes. He would then go back and improve his material. This young writer opted to listen to instruction. He did not suffer from the insecurity of continuously trying to defend himself. Later in life, he declared, "I didn't know how to write until I met Sherwood Anderson." One of the most helpful things Anderson did for his young protégé was to introduce him to his network of associates in the publishing world.

In 1926, this young man published his first novel, which met with immediate and great acclaim. This book was *The Sun Also Rises,* and the young author who wrote it was Ernest Hemingway.

You don't have to be old to be a mentor. All you need is a vision for your own influence to increase beyond the seventy to eighty years of your own life. A mentor leaves a legacy that others will follow and reproduce. That sort of legacy is an integral element of the mentoring process.

What does mentoring look like from the viewpoint of the mentored? I have mentors in my life. Often I will sit down with people who are very successful in business or other areas of leadership and ask them for their advice for my life. I ask them to gauge my performance, tell me where I can improve, and show me how I can communicate better. Sometimes they tell me things that I don't want to hear. These criticisms, however, are things that I need to hear. This kind of input never fails to help me grow and reach my full potential.

So here are a few words of advice for anyone who wants a relationship with a mentor, starting with how to choose an appropriate person to be your mentor. The first thing to do is to find out what you need to accomplish your goal. It is vital to identify the skill, knowledge, attitudes, or character you most want to develop so that you select a mentor who possesses these characteristics. Usually the person who matches up with the qualities that you have identified as most important to you is the type of person who is best suited to help you.

Another method to determine your needs is to take a personal inventory. People who want to grow as leaders must take inventory of themselves, paying particular attention to their inner lives. I do this every month. I personally assess where I am, what I am doing, my time commitments, the checks and balances that I have instituted to pace myself, and my reading habits. I ask myself where I need to improve in the areas of communication, relationships, and my capacity as a brother, son, and leader. I question myself about the areas in my life that I might need to change and my own internal attitudes that might benefit from adjustment.

Another element of considering a mentor is factoring in how much you are willing to sacrifice in order to have a mentor. There is no point in getting involved with a mentor whom you do not respect or do not want to hear from. You must be willing to engage with your teacher fully.

Having found your mentor, your attitude should be a willingness to learn from the mentoring relationship.

There must be a hunger within you for learning. Too often, we think that we know it all, have heard it all, or have seen it all. The question remains whether or not we are willing to do it all. As the one mentored you must be hungry to be a doer.

You should create ways for yourself to get closer to the person you have chosen as your mentor. When people come to me for counseling in various areas of their lives, I ask them, "Have you tried any of the things that I suggested you do?" When the response is either, "What things did you tell me to do?" or "No, I didn't," I know that those people are neither hungry nor interested. They just want a quick fix for their problems.

Therefore, if you are someone who wants to be mentored you must first learn to listen to and then practice what your mentor teaches. Apply what you are learning. A mentor cannot help anyone who is not determined or willing to apply what is taught. We can discuss theories until the cows come home, we can talk around problems until we are blue in the face, but unless we take practical steps to ensure our success and growth, we will never be the people we were intended to be. This can happen even if we have the most exceptional mentor ever.

You must not only be determined to learn, you must also be teachable. Having humility does not mean that you have to become a doormat. Humility really stems from becoming a secure person who knows and accepts himself or herself. Humility means that even if you have to accomplish difficult tasks and submit to someone's authority, you will still appreciate the mentoring process. When you are being mentored, keep your ears open, your eyes peeled, and your mouth shut. Listen and learn.

One of the keys to being mentored is loyalty. If there is one indictment of Western society in general, it is that loyalty is a rare commodity. Loyalty when situations get difficult, or when you might be tempted to take advantage of somebody who has invested trust in you, is absolutely essential to a productive mentoring relationship. Mentoring is a two-way street. You place confidence and trust in your mentor, and your mentor places confidence and trust in you. The mentor has given you time, wisdom, experience, input—often at the expense of his or her family life. At times the mentor has even shared with you his or her most private and personal thoughts. It is imperative that you never betray that trust under any circumstances.

Being mentored requires that you ask, learn, follow up, and grow. The two keys to learning are effective listening and reflection, after asking for and receiving information. Requesting input and then rejecting the feedback and the person who provides it is worse than simply not asking at all. Therefore, it is important that you are not afraid of the feedback. You should welcome it positively. Learning will often require follow-up, and this means developing action plans, then checking on progress, and then getting further assistance.

The by-product of this process is growth. How does this happen? Through input, positive response, training, and listening to your mentors, your vision and discipline get into better shape. Increasing your win factor as you venture into adulthood involves exposing yourself to new relationships that are happy, healthy, and positive in nature.

Does the foregoing accurately describe the people you are presently associating with? How would you rate these people in terms of optimism and success? Remember that there is a natural tendency to emulate those people we constantly surround ourselves with. While close friends and family members certainly play an important role in determining positive elements of our future, the most promising influence will usually come from strangers. The reason that this happens is because over a period of time, friends and family tend to settle into their comfortable little niches, and consequently, seldom have new or stimulating ideas or experiences to share. This is not to say that such relationships are not significant, but rather, within the context of increasing our potential, they may be less likely to stimulate us in proper ways.

The immediate reward that is gained from meeting new people and listening to their success stories is that you will be motivated to be more positive and adventurous in your own life. As you listen to these people, you may hear only a sentence or two that is actually capable of altering your limited views or perceptions, but often that is all that is needed!

Once you find yourself surrounded by the right people, you will automatically begin to expand your horizons. There will be a tendency to allow yourself to engage in unlimited thinking, which simply means that you have chosen to stop focusing on immediate obstacles and instead focus on the positive possible outcomes. Unlimited thinking enables you to get in touch with "the big picture," which is so essential to your success. Why? The reason is because all great works begin with a great vision.

As a young adult, how can you recognize those people who can influence your win factor and mentor you for success? Winners attract good fortune by recognizing and acting upon their own inherent characteristics and abilities. They do not dedicate themselves to anything that others think they should do or be. Instead, they allow themselves to follow their own inner promptings. Winners may occasionally lose ground, but they never lose the battle. Through it all, they hold fast to their own self-confidence and self-esteem. In all circumstances, under all conditions, these people are not afraid to use their own knowledge and to do their own thinking. Winners separate facts from opinions and arrive at their own conclusions. While they do not pretend to have all the answers, they are not inclined to play the "helpless little victim" role. These people do not blame others for their bad luck.

I have discovered that even a one-million-watt positive charge does you little good if you surround yourself with a million watts of negativity. If you are interested in progressing in life then it is time you also become aware of the incapacitating power of negativity and the people who spread it. There are two types of people in your life. The first will nourish you, and the second will drain you. There are those who will help you grow, and those who will stunt your growth. Toxic, draining people can drag down even the most determined, positive person and cause you to fall short of your potential. I believe that there are some people whose sole mission in life is misery dispersal. These people drive little toxic green vans around the neighborhoods of positive people and create problems. They will do anything to disrupt your journey to fulfillment.

Seek out those who empower you, who inspire and complement you, the people who enable you to see great possibilities for yourself. It takes an enormous amount of energy to attain your goals and to strive continuously for greatness. You really cannot afford to have relationships with people whose very presence drains vital energy from you. It is important to align yourself with only quality people. You should endeavor to surround yourself only with people who will enrich and empower you. These positive people will encourage you to transcend yourself and grow. You might consider this as sort of a support group, your pit crew for progress in your life. This group of people can strengthen you in moments of weakness and pull you up when you are down.

It is also important to surround yourself with people who share your vision and who are willing to support you in pursuing that vision. You cannot make it alone in your journey to success. Therefore, if you are involved in relationships that are not mutually constructive, especially if someone hinders your progress, then you must make a decision. Is it possible to transform the relationship in question into one that is healthy, or do you need to sever it? We all need someone to coach and mentor us through life. We cannot grow in a vacuum. We have to be willing to seek out those with wisdom and say, "I don't know what to do, please help me." At some point in our life, all of us are like the blind person standing on a corner, waiting for someone, our mentor, to lead us across to the other side.

It is important to realize that you and your friends are not joined at the hip. You must be prepared to acknowledge when a relationship has soured, and then dissolve it. It does not have to be an angry parting. Just make it clear that you have noticed that you are growing in different directions. Explain that your values have changed and that the goals and objectives that you and your friends have are different. The ability to break away from toxic friendships can make the difference between living your dreams and not pursuing your dreams.

Relationships are such an integral part of our advancement that unless we make changes to our lineup of relationships, we are going to remain exactly where we are—stuck in the rut of our current habits. The best method of launching yourself onto the next level is to connect with someone who is already living at that next level. This is true mentorship.

At times a new relationship with a mentor will open doors of opportunity for you. The primary focus of connecting with someone more successful than yourself should be to gain from their wisdom and inspiration. Getting a break should not be your chief objective in working with a mentor. Often, if you build a genuine association, then over time new opportunities will naturally present themselves. Focus on building a strong bridge with your mentor because the best relationships in life take years to build, but the positive results can last even longer. I have come to the realization that, to a certain degree, when the student is ready the teacher appears. I met a man named Ron when I attended a business conference where he was a speaker. I was impressed with his intelligence and articulate presentation. We became friends, and Ron began to notice qualities in me that I did not notice myself. Through his patience and example, he helped me reach a higher level. He has been a powerful mentor in my life.

I believe that as you grow in consciousness, you begin to attract people who enhance your growth. Be on the lookout for those people. They are the masters, the mentors and the people who see potential in you that you do not always see in yourself. Find those individuals who can observe your performance objectively yet positively.

We all need to have friends who hold our feet to the fire and challenge us. You need mutually enhancing relationships. As my relationship with Ron developed, he imparted some of his work habits to me. Seek out the sort of friends who help you work on your weaknesses, not just those who endorse your habits and congratulate you on your strong points. Many times people blame circumstances for their problems. Usually, however, it is the crowd that people associate with, not the circumstances we encounter, that makes the difference in our lives. Good circumstances with bad friends will result in defeat. Bad circumstances with good mentors will result in victory.

Begin searching for someone to stretch your perceptions about your life's possibilities. Look for people with winning attitudes. Ask those individuals to teach you for a few months. Enjoy the experience of growth with the aid of an example. Mentoring is used in many settings.

Although it is common to me in business, we see it in parenting. One of my dear friends told me that his goal for the New Year was to become a better father. He planned on attending a program at his local church to help him improve in this area. Mentoring is commonly used in educational environments, especially with at-risk students. Mentoring is also the basic principle behind Big Brothers Big Sisters of America, an organization that I have been associated with for several years. This organization practices one of the best-known mentoring programs in the country. Big Brothers Big Sisters is an organization of more than five hundred agencies that serve children and adolescents. I love this organization because its goal is to make a positive difference in the lives of young people, primarily through a one-on-one relationship with an adult. These adults work to assist youths in reaching their highest potential. The volunteer mentor and the youth make a substantial time commitment, meeting for about four hours, two to four times a month.

I remember an episode in my late teens when I was in college. I arrived at the start of the college soccer season feeling cocky until the new coach singled me out. "Breslin! One hundred push-ups!" would be followed by, "Breslin! One hundred sit-ups!" Then, "Breslin! Sprint around the field." I staggered back, drenched in sweat, thinking, "Who is this guy?" More push-ups, more sprints, more sit-ups, and on it went. I wanted to scream at him, to throw his stupid whistle over the fence, or even gag his mouth. He would continuously say, "Now we'll work on the basics." I remember feeling that I had been playing soccer for enough time to not have any need for that type of drilling. The coach would have me doing ball passes, kicking, and more basics repeatedly. He was definitely on my most-wanted list. It turns out that before too long, I realized what an impact my coach had in developing my skills to the next level. This coach always believed in me and our team. One weekend we were playing one of the best teams in the country. I remember saying, "Coach, have you seen who they've got on their team?" My coach relied, "No, I'm too busy looking at who I've got on mine." My coach was an incredibly powerful mentor to me at that time in my life. He not only helped me become a better soccer player, he also made me believe in myself as a person by always encouraging me, and that is the most important contribution that he made to my life.

Pat Riley is one of the greatest coaches in the history of the NBA. His Los Angeles Lakers basketball team virtually owned the NBA in the 1980s. Riley recruited players like Magic Johnson and made him great. He challenged his team to become one of the best in the history of the sport, and it did. The Lakers' greatness affected many others who were rising through the ranks, like the one and only Michael Jordan whose Chicago Bulls went on to win six championships in the 1990s.

Riley states in his book, *The Winner Within*, "You'll never rouse the winner within by making people feel they're a fill-in for sideline greatness." The best coaches, therefore, bring out the best in you.

I believe that right now you don't even know 95 percent of the people who will help you reach your dreams. They are strangers at the moment. Some people close to you will not help you because they know you. It is difficult for them to take the mental leap from where you have been and where you are to where you want to go. Don't get upset about that. Look for someone who thinks like you, someone to help you move to the next level of achievement. Do not involve yourself in relationships that undermine rather than support you in your pursuit of your goals. Find a mentor you can follow—someone you can confide in, who will push you along, equip you, and teach you. Always remain teachable, for following a mentor is one of the keys to eventually becoming a mentor for others.

Achieving Balance in Life

Garry Cobb

I Looked Happy but Lived an Unbalanced Life

I started dreaming of being a professional athlete at the age of seven. It started out with baseball because my older brother, James, joined Little League. I used to sleep with my glove and dream of being a Major League baseball player. I lived, ate, and slept baseball during those years. When I turned ten I played in my first football league and also played in a basketball league. I studied and did my work in school, but my mind was on sports twenty-four hours a day. Fortunately I was good, in fact I was very good, and this opened doors for me to college and eventually led to a career as a professional football player.

I spent nearly my every waking hour thinking, planning, and working on football for most of the year. We had an off season, but it was dominated by football as well. I didn't have the best relationships with my wife and children because my mind and heart were focused on football. If football was going well, then I was going well. If football wasn't going well, then I wasn't going well. That was a very unhealthy way to live. It took playing eleven years in the NFL, retiring, and taking a while to clear my head to realize that I was living a very unbalanced life. Fortunately, I wasn't addicted to drugs or alcohol like a number my teammates, but I was addicted to football.

I lived to realize that football is not everything in life. You shouldn't put all your trust in your career or profession because ultimately it's not worth it. Remember that your relationships with your family and loved ones will be there whether you succeed or fail. Those relationships will also remain long after you've finished your career. You've got to place more value on the people who love you and care about you as a person than you do on your career or business, which will use you up then spit you out. Thankfully, I was still a young man when I retired from the NFL, but hopefully I am now a wiser young man. The unbalanced life I lived in the NFL is one of the reasons I'm writing this chapter, "Achieving Balance in Life."

You Must Simultaneously Manage Different Areas of Your Life

I've seen many people who have succeeded in one area of life only to let something else trip them up. You are going to have to successfully and simultaneously manage numerous areas of your life in order to have a long, healthy, and fulfilling journey on this earth. It is extremely important that you use wisdom in your pursuits, and that requires planning. Could you imagine a builder not having a blueprint for a building that was on the verge of being constructed? That would be preposterous. You need to have goals and a game plan for your life. Your goals may change as you get older, but at least you've got something to use as a road map so you know when you're on the right path and on schedule.

Journeying to Your Senior Years

One exercise, which I think is very enlightening, is to imagine yourself old and retired. Yes, a senior citizen with most of your life behind you. Then I want you to become invisible, so you can visit your family and friends and hear what they're saying about you without them knowing you're there. Grab something to write with and close your eyes and imagine yourself listening to people talk about you and the life you've lived. What do you want the people who truly knew you best to say? Would you want them to dwell on your accomplishments?

Would you want your family to be able to recount specific times with you that were rewarding? Would you want them to mention loving comments you made that they will never forget? Would you want people to talk about how supportive and loyal you were? Or would you want your loved ones to have so little to say about you, that they would only talk about your career and accomplishments, as if you and they were strangers? What would you want the lasting image of you to be—the one your friends and loved ones bring up again and again? What would you want your friends to say about the way you've lived your life? Just talking about this exercise reminds you that loving your family and friends will help you put your life on the right course.

I encourage you to do this exercise on a daily basis for a couple of weeks, so you can establish some clear goals that will steer you toward living the type of life you want to lead. Put this all down on paper and you will have something to refer to when we talk about what type of person you want to be. Then I'd like to see you keep an eye on yourself by occasionally going back to check your notes to see if you're staying on course and heading toward being the person you imagined everyone talking about.

It Is Mandatory That You Plan Out Your Life

It is mandatory that you plan out your life with long-term and short-term goals. Many factors will be out of your control, but the things you can control should be managed in the way you desire. You need to intentionally decide how you're going to manage your time, ability, and money. You should take some time to think about these things rather than just living blindly from day to day. I encourage you to live your life rather than letting your life live you. Sit down and decide what you're going to do and what you're not going to do. In addition, you should think about where you're going to live and the close friendships you want to develop. I've heard it said, and it's very much true, that many people spend more time planning a birthday party than they do planning their lives.

Every week before each football game I played in the NFL we would put in a game plan for the particular opponent we were playing. You wouldn't dare go into an NFL game without a game plan. There would be complete chaos if you didn't decide which defenses you were going to play and which offensive plays you were going to run. A coaching staff had to sit down, meet, and plan a strategy for the upcoming game. The game plan was put together after the coaching staff watched hours of film on the opponent, then after taking into account the other team's strengths and weaknesses and our strengths and weaknesses, they decided on a game plan. If a team needs a game plan before a football game, how much more do you need a game plan for your life?

Time Management

Nearly every enterprise or undertaking in life is built on wise planning, which is solidified and supported through common sense. Planning also benefits immensely from your developing a solid and proven method of keeping abreast of the facts and following the progress of each and every facet of the undertaking or enterprise.

As far as I'm concerned, having a calendar and two notebooks is a must if you're going to be able to properly manage your time. Many people take on a large amount of responsibilities, which means balancing numerous activities and duties. Many people are going back to school while holding a full-time job, overseeing children who compete in some type of extracurricular activity, getting involved in social and leisurely activities, and are still trying to maintain relationships with a husband or wife and family. To do all of this requires a master personal notebook to write down all the things you're trying to take care of, a daily notebook to write down your daily tasks, and a calendar to keep track of your appointments and deadlines.

Daily System—Daily To-Do List, Master To-Do List

You should have a master list notepad. You should put as many items as possible on this master list notepad. That means everything you need to remember. If it's something you know you're going to need in the future or you think you might need in the future then it goes on the master list, regardless of what it concerns. Phone numbers, addresses, e-mail addresses, dates, times, you name it. Put them all down on the master list so you don't miss or forget upcoming events or responsibilities.

In addition, you should have another notepad to write out a daily to-do list. On a daily basis, preferably the evening before or in the morning, I sit down and write out a to-do list on a small notepad. On this list, I put down ten to fifteen things that I'd like to accomplish on that particular day. I don't like to write down any more than fifteen because a list too long can be discouraging. I like to be able to look at the list and see some light at the end of the tunnel as I'm going through the day. Unquestionably the activity I enjoy the most is crossing off the tasks on the list that I have accomplished. It makes me feel like I'm getting things done when I'm able to take my pen or pencil and scratch items off the list.

I don't know if anybody was more adept at managing and organizing than the former great coach of the Dallas Cowboys, Tom Landry. Coach Landry would go to management before every season and write out the formula needed to go to and win the Super Bowl. He would map out the time it would take in practice and how many minutes were needed in every area during practice sessions to reach the ultimate goal. He was the first to schedule practice by planning every minute we were on the field and exactly what we would be doing. The coach put together a series of plays and notes before each game. I encourage you to schedule and plan your days in much the same way Tom Landry scheduled his practices and games.

Don't Live from Crisis to Crisis

People who live a balanced life don't go from crisis to crisis. They take care of a problem before it becomes a crisis. If you're failing classes that's a crisis. If you have a weight problem and it's threatening your health, then that's a crisis. If your car's tires are so old and worn down that they're about to pop, then that's a crisis. If you're so late in paying your rent or your mortgage that you're at risk of being evicted, then that's a crisis. If you're bouncing checks like dribbling a basketball on the court, then that's a crisis.

I was brought up in a household where my parents never went to the dentist unless they had a toothache. They were not accustomed to periodically visiting the dentist for checkups. Their dental care was handled on a crisis-to-crisis basis. I remember seeing them in pain and agony as they tried to get into the dentist's office to relieve their suffering. I discovered that there's a better way to manage your dental care.

A crisis forces you to put the rest of your life on hold to take care of that particular situation. A crisis is an emergency. People who live a balanced life rarely get into crisis situations because they plan ahead. They generally do everything they can to avoid putting themselves in that position. These wise souls take care of things before they get to the crisis stage. A health crisis, financial crisis, or a relationship crisis will take your stress level up through the roof and have you getting old well before your time. It also can take the joy out of your life. On the other hand, balanced living that uses wisdom will allow you to enjoy all your years on this earth.

Prioritizing Is Putting First Things First

Prioritizing is your only way to ensure that you will invest the time and effort in the areas of your life that are most important to you. You don't want to be lying on your death bed and realize you invested your best efforts and most valuable time in areas of your life that in the grand scheme of things aren't that important to you. Many people commit themselves to a corporation and overwork day in and day out, neglect their health, barely develop relationships with their loved ones, then retire and receive a cheap watch on the way out the door. Then in less than a year after their retirement, they collapse and die from some illness that was brought on by their ill treatment of their bodies. That's not wise living. I encourage you to live a life in which you honor the principles that are dearest to you, first of all by doing the things that benefit your faith (if you're a religious person), your family, and your loved ones.

Another early step will require you to prioritize different areas of your life. Common sense would tell you that you don't have an unlimited amount of time to work with. You only have twenty-four hours in the day. You can't do everything that you might want to do or what someone might want you to do. You are going to have to select things to do that are very important to you. Everybody has a family life, social life, work and career life, financial life, and spiritual life. You have to decide what is most important to you. For instance, if you want to be a doctor, the rigorous studying is going to limit your social life. And it would be very difficult to be a world-class athlete and stay out all night every night.

Unfortunately when you observe most people in our society scurrying about aimlessly like chickens with their heads cut off, one can only surmise that "common sense is not all that common." Many of these people are trapped in chaos because they have failed to plan and are therefore letting life and the problems they confront write their daily agenda. This is a recipe for failure. If you find yourself in this predicament, pull yourself from the midst of it. First of all, do the end-of-life exercise, identify your lifelong goals, and make the accompanying plans. After doing this, work backward, moving from your lifelong goals to your long-term goals then finally on to your short-term goals.

You must decide to do some things and decide not to do others. The key in making those decisions involves selecting the tasks that are most important to you. If becoming a lawyer is your most important goal, you should write down all the things you're going to have to do in order to accomplish that goal. I've been told by many lawyers that reading is their main task and that the first year of law school is the most arduous of the three. Then look at the amount of time it's going to require on a daily, weekly, and monthly basis to get the job done. Once you write it all out, you will then be in a position to know how much time you're going to have for other areas of your life.

Then go back to other areas of your life, identify what's next in importance to you, decide on a goal in that area, and again designate the amount of time it's going to require on a daily, weekly, and monthly basis to achieve your goal. These goals are just like destinations you want to reach in your life. By knowing your desired destination you'll be able to decide what to do and what not to do. In other words, if you know your destination, you'll be able to virtually look at a map and chart your course to it. So you need to take the time, sit down, and decide intentionally what kind of person you want to be, what you want to accomplish, and what types of relationships you want to build during your journey.

You must put first things first. Is it more important to see another movie, talk on the phone all night with your friends, or spend some quality time with one of your loved ones? Unfortunately, many times the importance or lack of importance of some things become evident when it's too late. You've got to put first things first. A good question to ask is, "Will this matter one way or the other in twenty years?" Having a quality relationship with your mom, dad, sisters, and brothers will always be important. Youngsters, I'll also tip you off to the fact that the friends you have in middle school and high school will likely fade from your life. Don't betray yourself and your future trying to impress them. Instead, I would like to encourage you to develop your value system. If you're a religious person, your faith will help you decide what's important in your life. If you're not a religious person you're going to have to decide what's more important, your family or your career.

In the twenty-first century, with the availability of the Internet and all its vast, inexhaustible information, it's extremely important to be discriminating about which Web sites you allow your eyes and mind to focus on. Additionally, you have to keep an eye on the amount of time you spend surfing the 'net, instant messaging your friends, chatting in chat rooms, along with playing cards or video games online. In other words, it's very easy to waste away a day, week, month, or even a year doing different tasks on the Web. Use your resources and don't let your resources use you.

Your Core Principles

This brings us back to you and your core goals and heartfelt principles. I think you need to have a spiritual foundation for your life. I think you need to decide what you believe in. For your life to be in its proper order, you must live it based on some rock-solid principles and a clear vision of the kind of person you want to be. This all goes hand in hand with writing out your goals and charting your life course. You need to spend some time each day thinking about the good people and situations in your life that you need to be thankful for. I would encourage you to read some good, positive books that encourage you to appreciate your life.

Second, you should find people who are like-minded. There's nothing wrong with encouraging people and turning negative people into positive people, but you've got to have friends who help you recharge yourself. These should be people you enjoy being around, who are positive. I try to be around positive, loving people who have qualities I admire and are the kind of people I want to become. I'd advise you to do the same.

Executing Your Plan

After you've sat down and laid out a plan for your life, then set out to execute that plan using common sense. You must have a way of keeping track of the facts. You've got to be able to measure how well you are doing.

Are you on track or off track? Are you moving fast in accomplishing your goals or are you moving slow? It's important that you take the time to do an inventory of what you're doing in your life. Some people spend so much of their time and attention looking up the road that they don't focus on the here and now. Others look back so much, focusing on the past, to the point that they waste the here and now. You should plan the future and appreciate the past, but you can't become so enthralled with either that you don't focus on living a quality life in the here and now. Many individuals don't take account of what's happening with their resources, such as time, money, career, and relationships. They can hardly remember or don't know how they arrived at their present destination. This is not wise. If you are able to decipher how you arrived at your present location, you'll be able to change your behavior to get where you want to be.

My head coach in Philadelphia was Buddy Ryan and he was masterful in executing a defensive game plan. Buddy would arrive at the stadium already knowing where he was going to attack the other team's offensive pass blocking. Once the game started he would probe the opponent by calling a few blitzes. He would just study the blocking scheme the opposing team employed to block the blitz. Once the team showed its hand, he would start calling blitzes coming from everywhere. Once a blitz got there, Buddy was like a shark that smelled blood in the water. He wouldn't stop calling blitzes until the other team was totally defeated. You attack your task in much the same way.

Maintaining a Good Attitude

I could talk about many things in this book, but very few are as important as your attitude. Your attitude is how you view things. You don't choose your parents or your size or your face or your life situation, but you do choose your attitude. You decide whether you're going to look at life and it's predicaments in a positive or negative light. You can decide to look at what you don't have, what you haven't experienced, what others haven't done for you, or how life has cheated you, or the mistakes your parents made. You can look at the fact that the race of people your were born into has been robbed and abused and violated. You can choose to make it your life's goal to be consistently bitter about what happened to your people one hundred to three hundred years ago. Life presents so many choices. According to an old saying, a pessimist sees something wrong in every opportunity while an optimist sees opportunity in every problem. If you can poison somebody's attitude, in due time you can render that person totally ineffective.

Be a thankful person. Look for the good in your life and dwell on it, rather than looking at the bad and dwelling on it.

You can change your attitude in a heartbeat and it can change everything about your life. Your attitude could encourage you to fight on, or your attitude could force you to give up.

Maintain the Health of Your Body

You've got to take the time to maintain the health of your body. It should be a priority because if your body can't function, you can't function. You could be doing great things on your job or looking forward to a really nice vacation with your family or friends but have to cancel all of it because you weren't feeling well. An illness could shut you down to the point where you can't leave the house or even get out of bed. Remember to avoid crisis-to-crisis living. Maintenance is a far better lifestyle. This maintenance should include having annual medical checkups, exercising at least four to five times a week, and having a decently balanced and healthy diet, including at least eight glasses of water daily.

You Need to See Your Physician at Least Once a Year

Chances are that you won't have to spend an inordinate amount of time getting checkups unless you have some type of physical malady. But you need to pay your physician a visit at least once or twice a year. It's preferable that you have your own doctor with whom over a long period of time you develop an open, transparent relationship. Doctor and patient conversations are confidential so there's no reason to concern yourself about the content of your talks being shared with someone else. It's not a bad idea to question your parents about their medical history and the medical history of your grandparents. That family medical history is usually a major factor in your health prospects and it gives your doctor things to look for. Therefore, it is important that both you and your physician are aware of any potential hereditary health conditions.

Exercise on a Consistent Basis

You should make time in your life to exercise on a consistent basis. Exercise has long been confirmed by the medical community as a surefire way to keep your health at an optimum level. Most physicians say that you need to do some type of cardiovascular exercise for at least thirty continuous minutes for a minimum of four to five times a week. This type of exercise works your heart and lungs, as well as increases your metabolism to allow you to keep your weight under control. Your body works best when it is correctly processing and eliminating the liquids and foods you consume during your meals, and regular exercise helps to achieve this.

You Must Work and Be Active

You should spend a considerable amount of your time working, which also will require accomplishing numerous tasks under pressure. If you're in school, you should be reading and doing your homework each night, so that you're prepared for the next day of school or the next test. And if you're out of school you should be working on a job or looking for a job. In other words, if you don't have a job then your job should be *looking for a job*. You are wasting your life and your time if you wake up each day without any goals or ideas about what you're trying to achieve. If you're working, then you should be doing homework and studying how you can improve your performance. Regardless of whether you're still in school, you should be reading on a regular basis and expanding your knowledge. In fact, the more I live the more I believe you should spend the rest of your life going to school part-time. Things are changing so rapidly in our world that you've got to continue to be educated to keep up with your area of expertise. You should never stop learning or advancing your education regardless of your situation. If you are working, you can believe that your employer has a plan or agenda for the company's future. You should have your own plan for your future. How long do you want to work at your present job? What do you want do in your future?

Take Time for Leisure Activities

You should spend some time just having some fun. All work and no play won't just make Jack a dull boy, it will eventually make him a very angry boy as well. You should have some hobbies that allow you to just relax and get your mind off anything concerning school, work, or other responsibilities. I think it's good to develop hobbies in different areas that will support you in different ways. Going to the movies is a lot of fun and it allows me to take a mental trip into somebody else's world. I like to read books about different subjects and stories about things I don't normally get exposed to. You don't have to have a lot of money to enjoy your leisure. Spending a day in the park or at the zoo can be very enlightening.

Get Enough Rest

You must take some time to get the necessary rest you need to avoid becoming sick or burned out. Some of the most lethal conditions and health and mental problems in our society are linked to the chronic stress and burnout experienced by people who work. The ironic thing about working too long and too hard is that you usually don't work well. If you're rested and refreshed, you will be able to work more efficiently and get a lot more results out of your work. Your body and your mind require sleep and rest to revive themselves and continue to work effectively. You need to occasionally cut off all the stereos and television sets, then allow yourself to calm down and quiet your mind. Many of us are overloaded with news, facts, and voices. We wonder why we can't lie down and go to sleep. There's just too much noise in our lives.

Value and Maintain Your Relationships with Your Loved Ones

You've got to take some time to invest in the key relationships in your life. When was the last time you told your spouse, children, mom and dad, or brothers and sisters how much you love them? Many of the most important things in life don't sound an alarm when they are being neglected. Unfortunately many people procrastinate investing much needed time and effort into these valuable relationships until it becomes too late. You might not be investing enough time and effort in your relationship with your spouse or children. If you continue to neglect your relationships, there could come a time when a relationship is tested. This could be an illness or a setback of some type in your life or in the lives of your spouse or children. You or your folks may run into something that requires all of you to lean on the bond of trust and understanding that you have established between each other.

If your relationship is not where it should be, the situation might develop into a crisis predicament. That could very well require you to spend time trying to strengthen a relationship during some stressful and nearly impossible circumstances. This would be akin to putting a roof on a house during a thunderstorm. While it may be possible, it is certainly not wise. If you don't stop things from slipping to a crisis point, the job to fix them will require you to put other important things to the side and dedicate your attention, time, and effort to that specific task. If you live in a crisis stage for too long, it will jeopardize your physical health, your mental health, your meaningful relationships, and your future. One of the reasons for this chapter is to help people stay out of crisis situations by planning ahead of time.

I would advise you to spend some one-on-one time with each and every one of your immediate family members. It would be a good idea to find out what type of activities your spouse and children, as well as your father, mother, and sisters and brothers like to do in their leisure time. People tend to open up more when they're involved in activities they enjoy. Find out when they have some free time and plan an outing with them. This will give you a chance to bond and share experiences that will stay with you through the rains and storms of life. Many extended families only get together at funerals. And unfortunately some of the best things spoken about people are said when they're lying on their deathbed or in a casket. My mother always says, "Give me flowers while I'm living." This is a good way to live.

Accepting Personal Responsibility

Garry Cobb

In Your Life, You Are the Driver

Many times people will use the excuse that they did something because somebody else happened to do it. That isn't a good enough excuse. You are not in charge or responsible for what others do, but you are responsible for what you do. Responsible people aren't swayed by decisions others make. They're able to stand on their own and choose the proper response regardless of decisions their friends are making.

Let's say you look out the window and you see a car with five people in it drive by and go to the nearest light and take a right turn. Let's say the windows are down and you could hear the people in the backseat saying, "Take a left, take a left," repeatedly. Who decided that the car was going to take a right? The driver. Correct? Now let's say that same car was driving down the street and came to that same light. And the riders in the backseat said, "Go straight, go straight," and the car takes a right turn again. Who decided that the car would take a right turn? The driver. Yes, the driver was the individual who decided to take that right turn. Now let's say that same car came down the same street and the person riding on the passenger side said, "Take a left, take a left," as they approached the light. Yet the car takes the right turn again. Who decided that the car would take a right? If you say the driver again, then you are right again. I went through that story to say this one thing. *In your life, you are the driver.* You can have people tell you "to do this and to do that," but ultimately it is you who decides what you want to do. Right now, I'm a passenger in your car as you read this book. You can read everything I've written, but it's you who will decide in which direction to steer your life because you are sitting in the driver's seat of your life.

If by chance, you remember this book twenty, thirty, forty, or fifty years from now and you find yourself in a state of disappointment because you didn't live the kind of life you wanted to live, you can put all the blame on the person sitting in the driver's seat. If, on the other hand, you remember this book twenty, thirty, forty, or fifty years from now and you find yourself in a state of joy because you lived the kind of life you always dreamed about, you can thank and congratulate the person in the driver's seat. For it was the same hero or villain in the driver's seat who made all the decisions.

That is really what life is, it's a series of decisions.

The Ability to Choose a Proper Response

My definition for the word *responsibility* is "the ability to choose a proper response." Therefore, my definition for *irresponsibility* is "the inability to choose a proper response." Many times in our society, people shy away from personal responsibility because one of the elements attached to responsibility is *accountability*. Accountability means to be held responsible, liable, or answerable. That means that the person who is accountable for something is the one responsible if the wrong response is chosen. If something happens in a home, the adults or parents are going to have to answer questions about what happened, because they're in authority or in charge or responsible. If a baby or toddler gets injured, right away the police and medical personnel want to talk to the parents because they're responsible and are going to be held accountable.

I know a guy whose daughter drove a car that was registered in his name. She was working in Philadelphia, so she drove the car to work and received a large number of parking tickets because she parked illegally near her job. My friend knew this was occurring, but he failed to reprimand his daughter and force her to start obeying the law. Well, when they sent the parking tickets to my buddy's house, the tickets were in his name. He was the one held accountable for the tickets because the car was registered in his name. He was the one responsible. His daughter was the one who chose the wrong response, but it was her dad who was penalized for the wrong response. Since the car was registered in my friend's name and he let his daughter drive it, she's considered to be operating the vehicle under his authority, therefore he's the one responsible for her wrong response. You should realize that it's that way with your job if you're in a position of responsibility. If the people under your authority do something wrong, you are the one who is going to be held accountable for it. With authority comes responsibility.

Many times during my NFL career, I was the person in charge of running the huddle of the defense. With the responsibility of running the huddle, you were the one responsible for telling everybody in the huddle before each play the defensive alignment to be used. If a specific player didn't get the call, it was his responsibility to let me know he didn't hear it before he got in position to play. Each player was held accountable to know where he was supposed to be on each defensive alignment. If a player made too many mistakes and showed irresponsibility in his play, he was removed from the game. After each game we were graded on each play and given a plus or a minus, depending on whether we did our job or failed to do our job. We were given a report on how we played after each game. This was a method of accountability.

As a Teenager

Freedom is the side of responsibility that everybody likes, but accountability is the side of it that most people don't like, but they both go together. As youngsters grow up, they eventually mature so that they're able to start building relationships and activities, which they initiate, then monitor and maintain while their parents watch in the background. They start being able to stay at home by themselves and go places with their friends without adult supervision. That's a big step. If they show they can choose the proper response in those situations, they're given more and more freedom. Teenagers might even get to the point where they've shown they can choose the proper response so well that they can be left at home with no adults, and they're given the responsibility of watching their younger brothers or sisters. It might not seem like a promotion, but it is.

Another maturity step occurs when they get their driver's license and are able to get in a car by themselves and drive it wherever they please. This is another step of freedom and also another step in responsibility. They have to show during an actual driving test and a written test that they can choose the proper response on the road and be able to correctly operate an automobile on the streets of this country. With that additional freedom, they're able to jump in a car and drive anywhere they want, any time they want, as long as they continue to show the city, state, and federal authorities they can choose the proper response in any situation involving their vehicle on the road.

As an Adult

People's growth should continue, so that they eventually know how to choose the proper response to any situation, in much the same way that their parents are able to do. But that will mean being a self-starter. Self-starters don't need somebody to tell them to get out of bed in the morning. They take care of their own maintenance. Simple things like checking on their credit score, keeping an eye on their investments, seeing what can be done to make some extra income, are all things a responsible person does. They do these things on their own. They decide what they want to do in their lives, then they set goals and devise a plan to achieve their goals without their circumstances or anyone forcing them to do it. That's what needs to happen in a person's growing process.

People should get to the point where they know everything that's needed for all the areas of their life. They should have separate files and information for the different elements in their life. It shouldn't be necessary for circumstances to affect them before they look in their files and examine all of their notes and information about something that concerns them, so they can sit down and make the calls to get an appointment or whatever else is needed to stay on top of the goings-on in their home, at their job, or in personal relationships. People should reach a time in their life when they're able to handle extra duties at their job as preparation for a promotion.

Responsible adults don't have any one looking over their shoulder and reminding them that they have to be at an appointment on time. That should be something they take care of themselves. If they're responsible, other people should be able to count on them to fulfill their commitments. If they say they're going to be somewhere at a certain time, then they should be there when the clock gets to that time. But that means being able to choose the proper response to a situation by planning ahead of time and by being disciplined. It means ending meandering telephone conversations, turning off the television, and shutting down the computer.

When people reach this level, they're ready to get a promotion at work or take on more responsibility at home. Others will have confidence in people who can make the proper decisions in nearly every situation. They'll know how to chose the right business and social friends and how to decide which activities to get involved in and which ones to stay away from. For instance, when I was at USC some of the students tried to attend every party on campus. Well, in due time these students flunked out. Some of my teammates lost their scholarships after their grades fell because they were trying to go to every party on campus. The same is true if you're a business-person who has a long day of meetings approaching. Should you stay up all night looking at television or turn it off and get a good night's sleep? If you're the parent of a toddler, you've got to get rest so you can monitor what that child is doing. You may not be getting paid for it, but that's a job.

You Should Learn to Be Focused

Learning to be focused is another ability that is required of mature, successful people. A child can be distracted by just about anything at any time. Toddlers will drop whatever they're holding if you distract them. As people get older and more mature, they should develop the ability to focus on their task at hand and ignore all types of distractions. For instance, when driving a motor vehicle, people shouldn't become so engrossed in a conversation on their cell phone that they lose concentration on what their vehicle is encountering as they drive. People also shouldn't be turning around to hold a conversation with someone in the backseat or staring at buildings alongside the road.

In your work life, you should be able to focus on the tasks you're going to have to deal with in the upcoming week. It is necessary to be able to examine the minute details of your job. You should have a calendar and notebook and be able to focus on your schedule. You should be able to explain the details to someone else and not turn up missing when you have made a commitment to be somewhere at a certain time. A person with character doesn't flippantly throw around promises and fail to fulfill them. You word is your bond. Be willing to sacrifice to make your word good.

While I was playing football and the team would go into Giants Stadium in New Jersey, fans would be throwing beer on us and yelling profanities at us, but our job was to focus on what we were supposed to accomplish on each play. The coaching staff didn't care what the fans were yelling at you, all they wanted to know was that you were staying with the player you were responsible for. You had to be able to focus. Many times younger players would be taken out because they had trouble focusing.

Don't Rely on Excuses

Irresponsible people have a thousand and one excuses about why they're late or why something that was promised wasn't done. Responsible people do what they say they are going to do. They are willing to inconvenience themselves before they will inconvenience somebody else. Don't be the kind of person who comes up with excuses every time somebody depends on you to do something. Be willing to put your immediate desires to the back of the line and follow through on what you said you were going to do. Be the kind of person people can depend on to do what you said you were going to do.

Also, I don't like seeing people place all the responsibility for their lives on others. This is what irresponsible people who are refusing to mature do. They are getting older in years, but they're really becoming an older adolescent rather than an adult. For instance, if you've had four jobs and been fired from them all because of arriving to work late or not following the rules, this is being irresponsible. You may try to place the blame on somebody else, but you're the one who's really responsible. If you have done major damage to your car by driving it without oil, this is being irresponsible. You might be growing into an older adolescent. Failing to pay bills and ruining your credit are all signs of irresponsibility.

I had a teammate when I was with the Detroit Lions and he came to work every morning smelling like marijuana. He was a very good player, but he was fired and he was mad about it. Where should he place the blame? He should place it on his own head. I've had teammates who continuously were late for meetings and would then have the nerve to fall asleep in the meetings. Most of the time, the coach would fine them as much as five thousand dollars for five minutes. He would give them one chance and if the lateness continued, he released them.

You hear about these older adolescents on the news all the time. You know, people over forty, still living at their parents' home without a job. If you practice being immature as a youngster, you're going to be immature when you get older. It's much like playing sports where it's said that you'll play in the game the way you practice. If you're living like a spoiled, immature brat at the age of eighteen who depends on your parents the same way you did when you were ten, you're going to continue to live like a spoiled, immature brat as an adult. You don't get to a certain age and just grow up one morning when you wake up. It's a process, and somebody should start holding you accountable for your actions, because if they won't, one day the police will.

Responsibility Is Accompanied by Freedom and Accountability

One big problem in our society is that people want freedom but don't want the accompanying accountability. It's stressing our families, our communities, and our cities. In fact nearly everyone in the country is paying the price for people who want freedom, but they don't want the other part of it, which is accountability. For instance, when two people get together and have sex, they are exerting their freedom. If the female becomes pregnant, are the two people prepared to deal with the consequences that go along with having a child? Can they provide for that child without leaning on the rest of society? The odds are getting higher that they can't. That's why jumping into bed with someone for momentary pleasure without thinking of the consequences is irresponsible behavior. It's affecting our entire society because there are millions of kids being born to single-parent families that can't provide the guidance, emotional nurturing, discipline, and financial support for a healthy, happy childhood. These children grow up and wind up being problematic adults.

If You're in Charge, You're Also Accountable

Have you ever watched a school bus driver go out on his or her route before or after school? Well, the drivers leave on their route and pick up students and either drop them off at school or take them back home depending on what time of the day it happens to be. If it's in the morning the drivers take the children to school. If it's in the afternoon they take them home. If one of the children gets on the bus in the morning and doesn't make it to school, the first person the law enforcement authorities ask questions of will be that bus driver, and rightfully so. The driver had authority over that bus and the people on it. Therefore, that person should be held responsible for what happened to the bus and the people on it.

When that child gets on that bus, the bus driver is ultimately in authority or in charge. Whoever is in charge in a particular situation is also the person who is responsible. Being in charge means having authority over something or someone. Being in charge or having authority goes along with responsibility. If someone is not in charge or in a position of authority then that person can't be held responsible. For instance, your parents are in charge or responsible for what happens in your home. They have to make sure the rent or mortgage is paid, so they should and do have the right to set the rules. When you reach the point where you can move to a place of your own and pay your rent and mortgage on your own, then you can make the rules.

I have a bill that's due on the seventeenth of each month. If I don't make the payment, I'm hit with a late penalty that's fairly stiff. For far too many times, I have neglected to get that payment in the mail on time and I have wound up sending it as overnight mail, which costs about $15. I had to have a talk with myself because I was doing this month in and month out. This was just a lack of discipline on my part.

My Brother James and Yielding to Authority

My older brother, James, made the mistake of trying to make the rules before he could pay the bills.

When I was a freshman in high school, James came home from college for the summer. He was in his freshman year at Dartmouth College in Hanover, New Hampshire, and he was feeling somewhat independent. After all, James had been out on his own for eight or nine months and was used to coming and going as he pleased. Big brother James wasn't getting home many nights until three and four in the morning. He tried to hide this from our parents by not coming in through the front door but by climbing up the back stairs in the building where we lived and coming around to the boys' room, where the four boys in the family slept, and tapping on the window to wake me up. I would get up and open the window for him. James would slip on through with only my knowledge of it, or so he thought. Despite his trickery my dad and mom knew when he was getting home. This wasn't suitable for either one of them, so my dad had a talk with James and gave him an ultimatum. Get home by twelve midnight during the week or go live somewhere else. James had lived at home for eighteen years, and he didn't take it seriously. He let it go in one ear and out the other.

Well, about a week later around three or four in the morning, as usual, James tapped on the window. So just as I usually did, I got out of bed, opened the window, and let him crawl through the opening. But unlike the previous nights, before James could get all the way in, my dad was standing in back of me waiting for him to get his legs all the way through. Once James's feet were on the ground, my dad told my mom to pack a suitcase full of James's clothes. My mom started packing and crying. She was pleading with my dad to not put James out, but it was to no avail. My dad was adamant that my brother should go live on his own, since he refused to live by the rules they had put in place.

After my mom finished packing, my three sisters and two younger brothers were all awake. We couldn't believe what was happening, but we were all taking notice. James was being put out because he wouldn't follow the rules of the house. As my mom cried and hugged James, my dad shook his hand, handed him the suitcase, then told him to stay in touch because his mom would be worried about him. The rest of us stood there in our pajamas with our mouths open in disbelief.

Little did we know that my dad had called my grandparents across town and alerted them that James would be coming their way. Sure as day, James went over there and stayed for a couple of weeks before returning home after a bunch of apologies. He was as meek as a lamb when he returned and he always got home well before my parents' curfews. All of us learned that lesson right along with James. If you're not paying the bills, then you'd better obey the rules.

The Youth Study Center

I work with incarcerated youngsters as a volunteer at the Youth Study Center in Philadelphia. Many times these youngsters complain to me that they shouldn't be in jail. They argue that they didn't do anything criminal themselves, but they happened to be with somebody else who committed a crime. Unfortunately, I have to explain to them that in many cases they're going to held responsible for something somebody else did because they were with this person. If you're in a car and somebody in that car commits a crime, the police consider all the people in the car responsible. You should know the people you decide to befriend. If they're the kind who are involved in any type of criminal behavior, you could be held responsible for it, simply because you decided to hang around them. You are responsible for the kind of friends you have. You shouldn't jump into a car with anybody just because you know their names. You should know what kind of people they are, or you will run the risk of paying for it.

Deciding on who will be your friends is especially important. Regardless of what your age is, you are affected by the people you allow into your life. When you interact with someone, you wind up taking on some of their attitudes and beliefs, for better or for worse. You may not realize that someone is having an effect on you because it happens gradually. You can learn from these people. If you know somebody who has an issue that could mean trouble for you down the road, get away from that person. On the other hand, if you see a quality in a person that you admire and would like to acquire, then that's the kind of person worth spending time with. I'm not talking about fame and fortune, I'm talking about qualities like great character or being a great encourager or a person who overcomes tremendous adversities. You'll be inspired and improved by being around these types of people.

Jerome Brown and Driving at Alarming Speeds

I played with a great player when I was with the Philadelphia Eagles and his name was Jerome Brown. He was one of the greatest teammates I ever had during my years playing college and professional football. He played defensive tackle and he was outstanding at doing his job. But he also loved to drive his car at alarming speeds. I got into a car with him one time, and he gave me a ride to the football practice field. We must have been doing seventy or eighty miles an hour going down some small streets in south Philadelphia. I was terrified. Once we got to the field, I got out of the car and vowed that I would never ever ride in a car that he was driving. A lot of our teammates were laughing as if it were funny, but it wasn't funny to me.

About five or six years later, I was working on the radio as a talk show host on 610WIP, when a disturbing report came into the station. The report was about the death of Jerome Brown. He was in Florida and he was driving a Corvette in a rainstorm. The Corvette hydroplaned and landed on its roof and crushed both Jerome and his nephew. Jerome was in his mid-twenties, but he and his nephew were dead. We couldn't believe it because Jerome was built like a concrete building. Yet he was dead.

Cars Are Not Toys

Cars are not toys. They can easily be turned into killing machines, if you don't watch and pay attention to what you're doing. Don't play with your car. I repeat, it is not a toy. Thousands of youngsters die every year from reckless driving. If you've just recently gotten your driver's license, you should be slow to invite a bunch of your friends to ride with you, because they could easily distract you. Every year teenagers who have just gotten their license, go out on the road with their friends and have fatal accidents.

My Senior Prom Accident

When I was in high school I took my date to the senior prom in my dad's Ford Pinto station wagon. Unfortunately, while I was on the way to the prom I accidentally ran into the back of this gentleman's car. I wasn't paying attention when he stopped in front of me unexpectedly and I barely hit him. My date and I got out of the car and looked at the damage. It was hardly noticeable, but the gentlemen wanted to exchange our phone numbers along with our insurance information. So we swapped all the info and I promised that I would tell my dad and we would give him a call. We then said our good-byes and I headed on to the prom and had a good time.

When I got home, I dreaded telling my dad about the accident, so I just let it ride the next morning. It was on my mind that afternoon, but I let ride until the evening. Later that night, I was about to tell him, but I let it ride again. The next morning I was starting to think that the fellow I'd hit might have decided to forget about it since there was so little damage. So I kept my mouth shut, and a day turned into a week, and a week turned into a month. We were about a month and a week away from the accident when that gentleman called the house. You should have seen my dad's face on the phone when the guy told the story. I was in big trouble, plus the man was kind of upset that nobody had called him as I had said we were going to do. It all got worked out, but I wasn't driving that car for months.

You're in Charge of the MP3, Therefore You're Accountable for the MP3

Let's say you got an MP3 player for Christmas. If something happens to that MP3 player you shouldn't be able to go to somebody else and blame what happened to your

MP3 player on that person. After all it was your MP3 player. You should be able to keep track of that MP3 player. In addition you should be able to keep it in good working condition by guarding against its getting wet and by making sure to keep the necessary batteries for it to work properly. There's no reason why you shouldn't be able to read the instructions that come with the player and use it in the proper way. If your parents gave you some rules and boundaries regarding its use, you should obey those rules. For instance, if they say you can't listen to the MP3 at the dinner table or you can't take it to school, you should respect them and follow their instructions. You could listen to it or leave it whenever and wherever you wanted to within the parameters that your parents set up. If you misplace your player and then get mad at your folks for not being able to find it, you're acting irresponsibly and running the risk of this privilege being taken away from you. You should blame yourself for misplacing it, since you are the one who has authority over it.

Everybody's Got an Excuse

Humans are freewill agents, they can choose to do good things or they can choose to do bad things and then they will either benefit from it or suffer the consequences of it. But people don't like to held responsible for boneheaded moves, so some spend their lives blaming their upbringing or the way society treats their particular group. They act as if they had no choice and therefore were forced to do something, and they refuse to acknowledge that this was their choice. One of the common excuses is that they were raised in a dysfunctional family. They don't usually bring up the fact that most of the people brought up in dysfunctional families don't choose to be irresponsible. But the only way they can refuse to accept responsibility for what they did is to find a ready-made excuse.

Rather than blaming how you were raised or how the rest of society treats you, you need to accept that your decisions are your own. This is especially true in the United States where people can rise and fall depending on the choices they decide to make. Don't spend your life looking for excuses for every mistake you ever made. Take that time and effort and expend it on learning to make the right choices.

Don't be the kind of person who passes the buck or avoids responsibility. The psychobabble pushed by so many people in our society today provides a person with an excuse to just about every type of behavior: it's because of a bad childhood or a chemical imbalance or the person has been discriminated against. It's really disgusting to me when I see adults display no more maturity than a five-year-old child. If you become irate about something and go into a profanity-laced tirade, yet say that you couldn't help yourself, that's a lie; it's also childish and irresponsible. Life may hand you some really difficult setbacks, but you still have the ability to choose your response. Always remember that no matter how bad things get for you, there's somebody who has it worse.

Responsibility Equals Promotion— Irresponsibility Equals Demotion

You can look at your own personal freedom in very much the same way. If you govern yourself well and choose the proper response when you're given a certain level of autonomy, then in time you will be given more freedom and benefits. At the same time, if you abuse the freedom you're given, then chances are your bosses or the authorities will cut back on your freedoms and benefits.

One of the big factors that plays into living a responsible life is to intentionally develop good habits. The only way that happens is if you sit down and decide what kind of life you want to live. As you live you will develop habits and, unfortunately, if you don't make a point to develop good habits, you'll probably develop bad habits. For instance, it takes no effort to be a procrastinator, but it takes a great deal of effort to not be one. Try to avoid this by sitting down and deciding to intentionally develop certain habits.

Don't Rely on Excuses

You can't be considered a responsible person unless you hold yourself accountable for your actions. If you're late for school or for work, you shouldn't blame that on somebody else if you're a responsible person. People don't want to hear excuses. You can use an excuse for everything that ever goes wrong in your life, but that doesn't make it right and it won't help you to succeed. Achieving success in life means putting the excuses in a garbage can and finding a way to live up to your responsibilities. Unfortunately, too much of our society has become, for the most part, a blaming society.

One of the most important things your parents are trying to accomplish in raising you is to see that you develop into a person who exhibits personal responsibility. That means you have to take the reins in your life and decide what you're going to do each day. You have to learn to keep your hair and body clean. You must keep your teeth brushed and your clothes clean and neat.

Self-Discipline Walks Hand in Hand with Personal Responsibility

Don't be the kind of person who only deals with responsibility when you are held accountable. Those who behave in this manner can never be put in charge of something because they'll only act in a responsible manner if someone is looking over their shoulder. Responsible people would have to always watch this kind of person, and therefore that person can't be promoted. That means if you ignored or neglected something, such as completing a task on your job, and then got written up by your boss, he or she would probably not be inclined to trust you with more responsibility any time soon. You should stop living in an irresponsible manner and start keeping track of all your responsibilities at work before you have to be disciplined or before you wind up losing your job. The maturation process should result in your growing into a self-disciplined person who changes your behavior before anyone has to tell you to. Gaining the trust of your bosses takes effort and responsible behavior. Another term for it is *growing up*.

Maintenance Is a Part of Self-Responsibility

If you're consistently being given more responsibility at your job or your church, this is a sign to let you know you're walking in the right direction. On the other hand, if authority is being taken from you, then you've got to change directions. For example, if you have a car, but you don't drive it in a safe manner or you refuse to keep it up by making sure the headlights are working and the brakes are functioning properly, the police may stop you and refuse to allow you to drive the vehicle until you get it fixed. This is a great example of being irresponsible. I've noticed that many people fail to realize that most of their possessions need to be monitored and maintained. This takes time and commitment initially, but in the long run, you will keep your possessions performing properly much, much longer than if you had neglected them. If you neglect things like your home or your body, it will cost you much more later than if you were to take care of them immediately. Pay little now, but pay much more later.

Live in the Responsible Category

Make sure to live in the responsible category, because people who are irresponsible pay more on the back end than responsible people pay on the front end. Let's look at a parking ticket. The only reason you get a parking ticket is because you either didn't put enough money in the meter or you parked in a place where you weren't supposed to park. Being disciplined enough to not break the rules in parking somewhere can be inconvenient. You might have to pay for a parking garage or walk farther to your destination after parking. But you can choose to park at a spot that's convenient, yet illegal. You'll wind up getting a ticket and have to pay more money than any parking garage would charge. Irresponsible behavior always costs you on the back end.

People who don't take care of their health and procrastinate going to the doctor and getting checkups could wind up in a personal health crisis that will shut down their entire life. Many times people die long before their time because they weren't responsible about taking care of their health. Some people are irresponsible about preparing for their retirement or their children's education because they procrastinate year after year. They are selfish, thinking only of enjoying the here and the now. Regretfully, some people wind up dying in deplorable conditions because they refused to sit down and plan responsibly.

You Must Respect and Obey Authority

One of the keys to being a responsible person concerns knowing where your freedom begins and ends. If you've got a cell phone, you shouldn't be in the library or in church and let it go off and disturb everyone else. You shouldn't be walking into people while you're listening to your iPod. You should be watching where you're going and that may mean turning the iPod off and putting it in your pocket. Plus, you should respect and obey the people who have been put in authority over you, namely, your parents. If you work a job, you should be willing to obey the rules set up by the business owner.

If You're Not in Charge, Then It's Not Your Choice

I know a young lady who was working at a restaurant and objected to her boss's refusal to serve any more alcohol to a customer. The manager felt the customer was drunk and didn't want to run the risk of that person getting more intoxicated and causing an accident, which the restaurant owner could be held accountable for. This might cause the owner to lose his very expensive liquor license or cause him to be sued for millions of dollars. The young lady who was waiting the customer's table stormed into the manager's office and told the manager that if this person wasn't allowed another drink, she was going to quit. Well, you know what happened—she was fired on the spot and rightfully so.

She didn't have the power to make that decision because she wasn't going to be held accountable by the police and other authorities if the wrong response was chosen. The manager was the one in authority. Therefore, she wasn't respecting or submitting to the authority of the manager. In addition, she made the mistake of not recognizing where her authority and responsibility ended and where the manager's began. This showed a level of irresponsibility on her part, because she had chosen the improper response. She could have gone into the manager's office and requested that he review the condition of the customer and reconsider the decision to not serve him any more alcohol. But, it really wasn't her decision to make. Thankfully, her dad made her return to the restaurant and apologize to the manager. She didn't get her job back, but she learned a valuable lesson.

A person who has no respect for authority is irresponsible and not capable of being put in positions of authority. If you can't submit to authority then you're not responsible enough to be put in authority. Don't be the type of person who has to be made to take responsibility. Leaders govern themselves and their actions rather than having somebody looking over their shoulder.